If you've found
heavyweight car camping long on people
and short on nature—get away from it all.
Try lightweight backpacking.

The reason you go camping is to enjoy the outdoors and
take in the beautiful scenery, right? But lately it seems
that a lot of other folks have the same idea—and they're
doing it with fancy mobile campers, elaborate equipment
and all the comforts of home.

But there is a way to avoid the crush and the crowds.
Just put a pack on your back and take off on your own.
You'll be able to wander through unspoiled wilderness,
bathe in fresh mountain streams and experience the
adventures of secluded trails and rustic byways.

You'll need to know where to hike, what equipment and
clothing to take along, how to maximize your hiking
pleasure—and this book gives you all that important
information.

LIGHTWEIGHT BACKPACKING

It's the clear and easy guide
to the best way to enjoy the outdoors

LIGHTWEIGHT BACKPACKING

2 CUPS, 2 SPOONS, 2 POTS

For serious hikers who escape crowded campsites using a simple system of backpacking for a two-person team.

BY CHARLES JANSEN
ILLUSTRATED BY LINDA BENNETT

LIGHTWEIGHT BACKPACKING
*A Bantam Book / published by arrangement with
Robert Briggs Associates*

Bantam edition published March 1974
2nd printing
3rd printing

Published simultaneously in the United States and Canada

*Bantam Books are published by Bantam Books, Inc. Its trade-
mark, consisting of the words "Bantam Books" and the por-
trayal of a bantam, is registered in the United States Patent
Office and in other countries. Marca Registrada. Bantam
Books, Inc., 666 Fifth Avenue, New York, New York 10019.*

PRINTED IN THE UNITED STATES OF AMERICA

Table of Contents

Introduction

Tent Camping from the 1930's to the 1970's

My first tent-camping experience was as a boy scout in 1935 at a troop campsite on Lake Starette, Wisconsin. Eight scouts slept on canvas cots with three-blanket bedrolls in a huge patrol tent with stout wooden poles and numerous heavy rope lines. In an equally huge tent we ate well with food prepared over a large cast-iron stove.

Our troop swam at nearby Crystal Lake, a tiny, crystal-clear lake about a half mile long by three-quarters of a mile across, with a beautiful white-sand beach. I cannot recall seeing any established public campsites on Crystal Lake in 1935.

Years later, perhaps in 1951, my wife, Connie, and I, and our two small sons, Chuck and Tom, rediscovered Crystal Lake while vacationing at a nearby cottage. We drove down rutted gravel roads and came upon 12 families tent camping in a semicleared area amidst tall pines along the lake shore.

In 1969, when our family last camped at Crystal Lake, detergent foam ringed an arc of several hundred feet of shoreline and beach fires over the years had grayed the formerly sparkling white sand. There were approximately 380 campsites, each with four to six people. Expensive travel trailers dominated the shoreline with a sprinkling of motorized travel homes. Metal-bottomed, canvas-roofed campers were about equally mixed with large aluminum-framed tents. I felt almost apologetic in my inexpensive, lightweight, two-person mountain tent.

1

With 1,600 to 2,000 people sharing the campground, plus 100 to 200 picnickers on the other side of the lake, it seemed pathetic to me that these people who were motivated to "get away from it all" had ended up congregating in a virtual small village, with their generator-driven electric lighting, butane heating systems, refrigerators, radios, TV's, and hundreds of glaring lanterns. Campsites were generally littered and garbage cans overflowed. Newspapers were sold from self-service stands along the blacktopped street intersections.

This was getting away from it all?

Alternative to Car Camping for Serious Campers

Based on the curiosity exhibited over our tiny two-man mountain tent, sparse equipment and backpacks, I had the distinct impression that quite a few campers at Crystal Lake appreciated the simplicity and inherent freedom of our lightweight backpacking and would perhaps like to give it a try. Over the years other campers have expressed interest in our family backpacking adventures and our ability to pack up on short notice. This book is especially written to help serious campers make the transition from heavyweight car camping to the adventures of lightweight backpacking in a methodical, proven manner.

Over the years our family has developed a system of practical backpacking that is a composite of many good ideas from personal experience and numerous written sources. There are many systems of backpacking. Our system is so simple and has worked so well in so many situations that we feel it's worth learning, if for no other reason than that it will provide a basis on which to develop your own personal style of backpacking.

The system discussed in this book is based primarily on a two-person backpacking team, hiking in moderate climates during weekends or vacation periods of one or two weeks. Since our family is somewhat frugal, our equipment is meager and inexpensive, although functionally excellent. Our system of backpacking is easily adapted to various types and brands of equipment.

The system has worked for even-numbered groups of two, four, six and eight people. It has also worked for odd-numbered groups up to seven people, provided that one member of the group owns a three-person tent.

Motivation for Backpacking

There are two excellent reasons for lightweight backpacking:

1. Campsites are crowded in direct proportion to their distance from a road.

2. The finest scenery in the U.S.A. is to be found off the beaten path, or away from easily accessible roads.

This example may be helpful. Our family moved to Bellevue, Washington, about 10 miles east of Seattle, during the late summer of 1969. Camping enroute, we stopped off at magnificent Jenny Lake at the base of the Grand Teton Mountains near Jackson, Wyoming. Campsites were full and park rangers were suggesting sites of 10 to 20 miles away to carloads of campers who were visibly disappointed. By contrast, we drove into a nearby parking lot, put on our packs, and leisurely hiked 2.7 horizontal miles along the lakeshore to a dreamy campsite opposite Mt. Moran, where we were the only campers on sandy Leigh Lake. No problem at all getting a campsite, although admittedly it was badly littered.

Our only concern was a huge blackened ring of stones full of partially burned logs atop a pile of old coals. This obscenity was right in the middle of the sunlit sand beach. Garbage, burned and unburned, was sprinkled across the top of this monument to thought-

3

lessness. We dismantled the blackened rocks and timbers and randomly threw them into the woods. Next we buried all the coals. Finally we burned the unburned garbage on a tiny three-rock cooking fire we made in the woods and packed up all the burned garbage in a plastic bag. When we left, there was no sign that anyone had ever camped there. So it should be everywhere.

Backpacking May Be Modest in Scope or Ambitious

Son Chuck backpacked throughout Europe and the Middle East for about one year, living on 80¢ a day, although, as he says, "You've got to like bread and fish."

Sons Chuck, Tom, Dick and I circled the Tetons in 1967 on an adventure-filled 67-mile backpack trip with a total budget of about $300, which included round trip rail fare (steerage class) from Elgin, Illinois, and a clean motel room in Jackson, Wyoming, for the first and last nights of our vacation.

Our equipment at that time was sparse and handmade. Two of our packs cost $8 each. The other two aluminum packframes used on this hike were handmade from discarded aluminum lawn-chair components found in a junkyard. Our frames, which were modeled after the Himalaya Frame, cost about 40¢ for sheet-metal screws. Each packframe took me one week to fabricate. Packs were old Scout Yucca packs extensively modified by Connie. Packframe and pack weighed a little under four pounds, which wasn't too bad for an initial attempt at pack manufacture. The screws alone must have weighed ½ pound.

Our boots were unlined leather workmen's shoes with crepe rubber soles; one pair lasted me four years. Three of our sleeping bags were rectangular, the other one was a mummy bag. All bags were Dacron insulated.

4

Little Hikes and Big Hikes

Connie and I have backpacked from the front door of our former home in Woodstock, Illinois, to a tiny wooded valley known as Maas' Woods, only 2½ miles away. Neighbors eventually became used to the sight of two alpine refugees trudging down the street in their hiking clothes and backpacks. Once we went camping in midweek, and left the campsite at 5 A.M. so that I could catch the 6:23 A.M. train to work in Chicago. Another time we fried bacon and eggs in our stainless steel cups just to see if we could do it—we did. Still another time we deliberately omitted foam mattress pads and slept on the spring ground to learn if it were practical. The ground isn't soft, even spring ground, and we never did that again. Generally we had fun, and I suppose that's what backpacking is all about.

Connie and I have been a "mite confused" (the initial stage of becoming lost) on a 61-mile backpack that eventually ended in Stehekin, Washington, permanent population about 35. A 23-mile road along the Stehekin River serves the area, which is the gateway to the new North Cascades National Park. The concessionaire's daughter, Maria Byrd, came upon us just as we stumbled from 18 miles of dusty trail onto the main road, assisted our benumbed bodies into her taxi-bus and gave us a ride to "town." At that time we didn't carry cash or checks and were fortunate to obtain a room on credit in the lodge, where we took two baths apiece to remove the grime. Not having money for a longed-for meal in the restaurant, and not having courage to ask for credit again, we heated up something in our cooking pot but were too tired to eat. We made lemon tea and sat watching the bending river and lake as daylight quietly turned to evening.

The North Cascades National Park can be reached only by boat, floatplane, horse, or foot. There are no telephone or road connections with the outside world.

Emergency communication is made by radio. Well-dressed tourists and bearded hikers intermingle at the lakefront boat dock; tourists sit at the lakeside restaurant eating hot lunches, looking down at bedraggled sunburned backpackers who are slowly nursing the last calorie from their leftover tins of sardines, each group a bit superior to the other. All await the 50-mile four-hour boat ride back to civilization. Hopefully, all recognize the uniqueness of Stehekin, port of entry to wilderness.

What to Expect

Our family has been cold, cool and hot, drenched, damp, and too dry, becalmed and all but blown off the ground. We've dragged our nonresponsive bodies slowly uphill in a half day, and virtually sprinted (well, almost) 18 miles in a full day. We've sat along the trail, flopped along the trail and once at 11,000 feet in the Rockies, Connie collapsed on the trail.

We've hiked mile-high trails winding hour after hour through flowering alpine meadows in Grand Parc at Rainier National Park, and we've sat quietly all day watching the ever-changing face of water and rock at Spencer Spit on Lopez Island in the San Juan Island group of Washington State.

Adventure from Midwest to Northwest

We are proud of our many adventures and want to share our slowly accumulated expertise with you. Neither Connie nor I nor any member of our family has ever hiked higher than 11,500 feet, but we have all backpacked to and camped at 11,500 feet.

We have never camped in hotter than 100-degree weather and never colder than 10 degrees below zero. We really didn't want to camp below zero, but while Chuck, Tom and I had enough money for ski-lift tickets, we didn't have enough money for a motel room.

6

So on a bright moonlit January night, enroute to Indianhead ski area in Michigan, we tent camped at Crystal Lake, Wisconsin, where it was very quiet, very cold, and not too crowded.

We have never fallen off a cliff; well, Dick did once when a refrigerator-size rock to which he was clinging decided to disassociate itself from the rest of the cliff; yet it was only once, and he was expertly belayed by our friend Steve Zimmermann, now in college at Rockford, Illinois. While dangling, Dick may have acquired some new goals in life, as I noticed he leaned more toward canoe camping and swimming after that experience.

We have never swum across a raging torrent with our packs, but all eight of us have canoed across a raging lake in Canada with our canoes lashed together, catamaran style, to keep from overturning in the high wind and waves. Jean was four years old at the time and sound asleep in the canoe bottom with her teddy bear peering out from the flap of her tiny pack.

Safety Is An Attitude

Unlike grizzled veterans, I see no reason to apologize for the fact that in 13 years of trail, canoe and rock hopping, not one member of our family, nor any one of the friends who have camped with us has ever fallen to his death, been seriously injured, frozen, burned, or permanently lost. We believe in and practice safety, on and off the trail. Accidents can and do happen, but many so-called accidents are caused by placing your fragile body in places and situations where statistics and common sense are no longer on your side.

In our amateurism we frequently quit, back down, change routes, and do something other than what we had originally planned. On an early-spring hike we didn't push on and trek uphill for eight lineal miles in the snow. Instead, we spent one extra day in camp and finally took the time to do all the glissading (sliding downhill on boot or bottom) we had always wanted to do. We skied, turned, flipped and flopped,

7

but all on a safe, flat runout totally void of body-destroying boulders.

Join Us

We hope our book enables you to profit from our simple system of lightweight backpacking and helps you make the decision to venture forth on any one, or many, of the thousands of wilderness trails throughout the United States.

A Chinese proverb appropriately says, "The longest journey begins with a single step."

So let's begin.

Philosophy

Pack What Is Necessary

Sons Chuck and Tom were seated around a campfire near Longs Peak, Boulder, Colorado, in 1968 when
a lonesome hungry climber from another party
dropped in for talk and an apres-dinner snack. Tom
offered their guest some surplus dried prunes. Obviously a lightweight purist, their climber-guest quickly
reacted with horror, "You backpacked the pits?"

The name of the game is lightweight backpacking
and this means you only pack what is absolutely necessary. The prune pits were not, and their needless
weight adds up. A companion to light weight is low
volume; both are essential to backpacking, as your
back and pack will only hold so much, at least for
comfort.

Gain More with Less

As the camper-turned-backpacker becomes more
serious, he slowly realizes that by ridding himself of
needless possessions he gains greater freedom of movement and mind. With less he actually gains more. It
isn't necessary to own an expensive mountain chalet,
as the most humble backpacker seated on a tiny knoll
in a national forest "owns all he can see," to quote a
most meaningful Japanese proverb. He has a choice
of views from thousands of knolls in hundreds of forests in many states. Eventually the knowledge seeps
into our conditioned minds that *most does not neces-*

9

sarily mean best, neither does bigger mean better, nor does expensive mean more valuable. Too much camping equipment prevents mobility and choice; meager backpacking equipment permits mobility and the choice of the finest scenery and adventures in the United States.

Mood of Wilderness Backpacking

In the quiet and solitude of wilderness some very basic thoughts emerge as to who we are, and why we are, and where we are headed. Some of the mood of wilderness backpacking may be captured with a few fleeting thoughts.

Joy is a child, and a child is simple.

Joy is tranquil, unhurried. Joy is a million blinking stars shyly emerging from eternity.

Joy is a liberated drop of water, cooled by its parent snow, caressed and filtered by the forest, dripping from an eroded granite niche, sparkling as it hesitates to fill your waiting cup.

Simplicity is sensing.

Feeling the powerful muscles of your legs carrying you higher and higher. Counting rings on a Douglas fir sawed by an unknown woodsman; realizing that the quiet giant was a seedling in 1622. Breathing the cool air of the shaded forest, the sharp scent of brown-dry needles from fallen pine, the gentle fragrance of majestic cedar humbled and splintered by a massive snowslide, the silent damp of waking morn.

Delicate balance, stable rock underfoot. Resilient moss, pillowing dusty trails. Tense, hard, glassy ice steps. Hot rock, warm marsh, stiflingly humid flowering meadow. Flesh-numbing streams and bone-chilling alpine lakes.

Simplicity is being. Breathing, pounding, beating of temples. Sharing, looking. Aware, silent. A speck in time.

Simplicity is tea. Snow cones. Silence.

Simplicity is faith. In yourself, in your partner, in God, in tomorrow.

Simplicity transcends. Pot-seared finger, bleeding blister, disappearing faint trail.

Simplicity is a mummy bag. Soft, warm, protective, enveloping, quiet, sun-dried, waiting.

Simplicity is peace. Dull orange embers, fresh clean socks, mosquito netting, sunsets, cool air, guardian black firs silhouetted against dim turquoise sky. Morning sunlight on your tent, sleepy eyes peeking from hooded bag, slow smile, orange juice, today.

Simplicity is love. Memories of home, kitchen, and fresh salad. Trails end. Liberated feet. Car that starts, root beer milk shake, music. Children, telling, shower, letting down.

Simplicity is knowing when to stop.

Boots, Socks and Feet

Hiking Boots

Backpacking involves walking, and since you are serious about making the transition, the first order of business is hiking boots. Tennis shoes and old beaten up dress shoes are not good trail-hiking boots and are best forgotten. Workmen's-glove leather, crepe-soled work boots and "waffle stompers" are perfectly acceptable for beginning hikes on level city streets, dry meadows, and groomed trails; however, they are a poor substitute for hiking boots, particularly as the trail grows rougher.

Before descending on your local camping-shoe store, it might be well to trim your toenails square across so that you will get a true feel of your prospective new boots.

Most shoe stores will lend you hiking socks to wear when trying on boots; or you might bring along a pair of socks just in case your store doesn't participate in a lending program. Most hikers wear one pair of thick socks (listed by name in order of increasing thickness and cost): athletic socks, hunting socks, climbing socks, and ski socks. Some pairs are short and some cover the calf; that's your choice. In cool-weather hiking a warm calf is an efficient machine. In hot-weather hiking a long pair of socks is intolerable. Since you normally wear one pair of socks when hiking, I suggest your wear one pair when trying on new boots. Two pairs of socks soften and conceal points of pain in a boot while you are in the store; later, when you hike in one pair of socks, you'll discover those

13

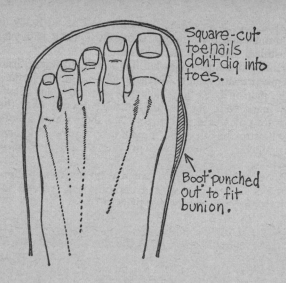

Square-cut
toenails
don't dig into
toes.

Boot punched
out to fit
bunion.

square cut Toe nail.

points of pain. Well-fitting boots worn over two pairs
of socks will be too large when hiking is done in only
one pair of socks. Most of us will not be hiking in
conditions so cold as to merit two pairs of socks. Socks
should either be fine woven wool, or Orlon, or a combination. Cotton is cold and miserable.

Fitting Boots

When trying on new hiking boots do not pay any
attention to preconceived notions of dress-shoe size and
width. Try on many brands, styles, sizes, and price
ranges, and if boots initially hurt, my experience has
been that they rarely get better. Conversely, a well-
fitting pair of boots generally fits from the beginning.
Eventually, in the fourth or fifth shoe store, you
should find your boot. You'll know.

Daughter Sharon has a high arch and shoe fitting is

difficult. Last year she tried on 15 pairs of ski boots in all brands and price ranges. None fit. On the 16th pair she smiled. She knew. So will you.

Hiking boots fit somewhat like a pair of gloves; firm, but no pressure points. Occasionally an otherwise fine-fitting pair of boots may have one pressure point. Carefully mark your boot on the outside, directly over the pressure point, and take it to a ski shop where a boot may be stretched *at a specific point* by a process known as "punching." Great for providing needed bunion room.

Boots that fit well but are a bit full from bottom to top may be fitted with a carefully cut padded insole, or thicker socks, or two pairs of socks.

What to Look for in a Boot

Height of boots is fairly critical as boots much higher than six to seven inches may rub your leg, and for some hikers will partially constrain ankle bending.

Gussets should fit snugly to prevent water from seeping in. No gaps permitted. Tongues should be well padded, especially at the top, where you lean into them. A padded cuff, known as a "scree cuff," is a nicety that supposedly keeps out scree (loose sand and pebbles); it doesn't, but at least it feels comfortable.

Speed lacing is nice, but not essential to a good fit.

Hiking boots have stiffer soles than dress shoes to prevent rocks or roots from bruising your feet. Leather uppers are heavier and stiffer so that you will not twist your ankle. Degree of stiffness is expressed in weight (pounds and ounces). You'll find lightweight hiking boots suitable for city hikes on paved roads; medium weight hiking boots suitable for most trail and snow hiking and stream wading; heavyweight (climbing) boots are generally used for hiking or climbing rock, snow and ice.

If you compare hiking and climbing boots side by side you will notice that the climbing boots have a thicker leather sole (stiffer), although both boots have the same thickness of neoprene-cleated (synthetic rubber) soles. Neoprene-cleated soles are currently sold in three grades:

1. A soft grade, taffy colored, identified as "Roccia," made by Vibram.

2. A medium-hard grade, black colored, identified by a black inset molded into the instep, marked "Montagna," made by Vibram.

3. A very hard grade, black colored, identified by a yellow framed inset molded into the instep, marked "Montagna," made by Vibram.

Grades 2 and 3 are the same thickness, while grade 1 is a little thinner. The yellow-marked Montagna sole by Vibram is the longest wearing and least likely to tear out on a sharp rock. That's how it is now.

NOTE: Dress shoe, 1 layer of leather; hiking boot, 2 layers of leather; climbing boot, 3 layers of leather.

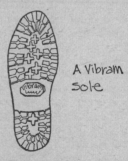

A Vibram sole

According to a reliable source, Vibram may shortly produce neoprene soles in one grade only. Since Vibram is distributed worldwide, this means boots purchased anywhere will have the same quality soles.

Vibram neoprene soles are attached to new and old boots by two different methods:

1. New boots: Neoprene soles are cemented directly to leather soles.

2. Resoling old boots: A subsole of neoprene or nylon is first cemented and stitched to the leather sole. Next, the replacement sole is cemented to the neoprene or nylon subsole. This system has the least technical chance of delaminating.

Both attachment systems screw or staple the toe of the Vibram sole to the leather sole. Obviously a screwed sole is handy if the sole has delaminated, since the screws are the only thing holding the sole in place.

In my opinion a yellow inset Vibram sole (Montagna), with screws or staples, cemented to a subsole of neoprene or nylon, with subsole cemented and stitched to leather soles, would represent the finest boot technology, although this is not yet available in new boots.

Assuming your boot soles delaminate, you may request and get a subsole of neoprene cemented and stitched to the leather soles. New Vibram soles and heels are then cemented to the subsole, which will provide you with better boots than you had originally. Boots are expensive, but they have many lives. First-class resoling as described costs about $14, which is one-half to one-third the cost of a pair of new boots.

Dress shoes have a welt that projects out from the uppers. Hiking and climbing boots also have a welt, but it is about one-half the projection of a dress-shoe welt. Small projection is stiffer and safer as it bends less if you are stepping on a precarious foothold.

Stiffer boots are not inclined to bend much, so intelligent shoe manufacturers have various means for the boot to bend slightly in the heel, or at least I think they should.

Most medium-weight hiking boots, and particularly all heavy-weight climbing boots, will be leather lined and some will be padded inside much in the manner of a ski boot. In moderate to cool climates this is a desired feature, assuming that the boots fit in the first place. In warm and hot climates lined or padded boots will parboil your feet and should be avoided.

For most backpacking we are discussing in this book

medium-weight and medium-priced boots with either black medium-hard or yellow very hard Vibram Montagna neoprene-cleated soles are suitable for general backpacking. Heavier weight (climbing) boots are more boot than you may initially need. You can always graduate to a heavier and more expensive pair as you develop expertise and learn what is best for you.

Boot Waterproofing

Remove boot laces and rub suitable waterproofing into the entire exterior of your beautiful new boots, particularly into all seams and stitching. Boots will emerge rather dark and evil-looking, but decidedly waterproof. Be sure you use a recommended waterproofing for the type of leather cn your boots. My boots are "chrome tanned," therefore I use "SNO-SEAL." Your boots may be different, so determine their pedigree and use *only* recommended waterproofing compounds.

Strong Laces

While your laces are out you might place one lace around your booted foot and pull on it, trying to deliberately break the lace. If it doesn't break, place it back into your boot; however, it probably will break and should be replaced with soft nylon ski-boot laces, about ⅛-inch thick. You will have to depend on your boots, so they might as well be first class. I prefer a red lace, as it lends a bit of shmaltz to an otherwise clunky pair of boots. Black or white nylon ski-boot laces are also available, if you like black or white. I don't.

Do uneven laces bother you? They bug me and I solve the problem by centering the laces between the bottom D-rings and securing the loops with tight square knots.

Laces that are too long just hang there and do not

seem to know what to do. I've tried various solutions for shortening laces. Easiest is to cut out the surplus from the middle portion of the lace and tie the two parts together at the toe, between bottom D-rings with a square knot or fisherman's knot. This method both shortens and centers the lace, as the knotted lace is prevented from slipping out between the bottom eyelets, or D-rings. Remember that you are cutting a nylon lace, and be sure to fuse loose ends by holding the cut lace briefly over a burning match. Do not touch the hot melted nylon; well, at least you never will a second time, as it produces a burn you will remember. Second method of shortening laces is to double tie your bows so that your boots resemble those of a stubby cheerleader with pompoms. I favor the first method, which should be obvious!

New boots will try very hard to please their new owner, so carefully fit the gussets and tongue each time you put on your boots and you'll soon have them trained. If you don't do this you'll get a wrinkle in the leather that is impossible to correct and which inevitably will not hurt until you are well along the trail. Revenge from a boot treated poorly in its childhood.

Now that your new hiking boots are beginning to get broken in, you will be going on short day hikes and may end up by a campfire. *Never,* repeat *never,* dry out your boots by a fire. The leather will shrink and boots will hurt your feet forevermore in direct retaliation for roasting them. Sorry, but soaking shrunken boots in water will not bring them back to their original comfortable fit. Merely standing around a fire warming your toes is all it takes to shrink and ruin a pair of boots. I know, I've done it; no need for you to experiment and harm your boots. If your cold toes need warming by a fire, remove your boots so that the heat can reach your toes.

Wet boots are dried by wearing them and letting body heat and air temperature slowly dry out the leather. Dry socks will absorb more moisture than wet socks, so if you inadvertently soak your boots, remove the wet padded insoles and wet socks and put on a dry pair of socks to help absorb the excess moisture from the boot. Classic stream-crossing technique is to first remove socks, put your boots back on and then wade across the stream. On the other side, remove boots and water, put on your dry socks to absorb dampness inside your boots, and replace your boots.

Wet grass, rain, and snow will have little effect upon well-fitting Sno-Sealed boots. Normally boots get soaked by slipping off a stepping stone in the middle of a stream. If you are the unsteady type you might anticipate disaster and first remove your socks and then put your boots back on before tottering across stepping stones. Eventually you'll learn to move quickly and lightly across streams so that it will make little difference whether you are in the water or on the rocks.

My worst foot dunking occurred when I gallantly tried to assist Connie across a stream. She slipped, grabbed me, knocked off my glasses, pushed me off my dry, happy stepping stone and generally caused gloom and ugly mutterings. Future small-stream crossings witnessed a liberated woman nervously crossing on her own while I never looked back; after all, to quote Chief Blackhawk, "It's only water!" (see *Shining Trail* in Related Books section).

Eventually all backpacks come to an end. Boots should be dried at room temperature, away from registers and radiators. When dry, they should be brushed clean of dried mud and Sno-Sealed again so that they are ready for the next trip. Based on one sad experience, I would suggest inspecting your boots for signs of delamination between leather and Vibram sole. Store boots in a dry place. Since unheated basements are notorious for rotting leather, you would do well to store your boots upstairs.

Used Boots

Old boots have value, as they may be sold or traded for new ones. A high-class boot with one season's wear may have a trade-in value of a little less than half the original cost. This brings up the interesting fact that a frugal backpacker may be able to buy a high-class pair of used boots for a little more than half the cost of a new pair. But don't count on it. If you do find a pair, missing lace hooks may be installed in any ski shop. Son Chuck was fortunate in finding an excellent pair of used boots that fit him well. I forever look but never find a pair that fits me. Used boots have the advantage of being broken in and they also offer instant class—you're a veteran, right now!

On the other hand, why wear a pair of boots that don't fit even if they are free? Boots are the only thing between your delicate size 12's and sharp roots, jagged stones, wet snow, cold ice and hot coals. Select your boots carefully, break them in properly, treat them kindly, and they will take care of you.

Socks

Foot comfort is not only dependent upon boots, but to a large extent upon the socks you wear. You will hear all sorts of sock suggestions as you shop for your first pair of boots. I too have a few observations on the subject.

Coarse-woven socks placed next to your foot are painful, as the weave will press into the skin, marking your feet like a hot waffle grill. Fine weaves are excellent; coarse are painful. Cotton socks absorb perspiration, hereafter called "sweat." Damp cotton socks make your feet feel cold. Wool socks feel warm when wet; Orlon socks feel warmer when wet. Wool dries slowly; Orlon dries quickly. Sometimes wool socks matt and shrink when washed; Orlon socks do not. A happy compromise is a wool-Orlon blend.

Tight-fitting stretch socks cause pain in your big toe. Tight-fitting socks also feel colder. Cushion-sole socks (double soled) are generally more comfortable than two pairs of single-soled socks. Most of my hiking is done in a light pair of Orlon cushion-sole socks, or I may use a medium-thick wool-Orlon ski sock. For cool weather I favor a pair of calf-length wool-Orlon climbing socks. I rarely wear two pairs of socks; no one in our family does.

Darned socks, socks with thin spots, or socks with holes have no pity on a backpacker. Wear them when your rich relatives, pastor, or boss are visiting.

Carry a spare pair of socks and change into dry socks (they don't have to be clean) each night before going to bed and you'll never have cold feet again while sleeping. If time and conditions permit the luxury of rinsing out your socks, then by all means do it, but be careful to not end up with a pair of wet or damp socks just before rainy or cold weather. Better dirty and dry than clean and wet. Socks aired in the wind and sun are *functionally* as good as freshly washed socks. Just fluff them up a bit.

Rinse Your Feet

Take the time to rinse your feet and legs once each day, if possible. Lunchtime near a stream is ideal. At the end of a hot day I've tried snow rinses, which work well as body heat melts the snow. Keeps you humble. Dry your feet with air, sun, or on sun-warmed rocks as you cannot afford the weight or bulk of a towel.

Flooded mountain lakes or streams frequently overflow into shallow depressions which, heated by the sun, make excellent bathtubs. Enjoy the 80-degree water while admiring the nearby snowbanks. But please don't punish your benefactor by using soap or shampoo; Madison Avenue will survive a few omissions of the American antiseptic-body syndrome. Rinse, don't soap.

Develop sensitivity for beautiful life-sustaining mountain water.

Breaking In New Boots

Break in your new boots and socks in the house, with short walks alone, or with your dog enroute

22

to your neighborhood store. Gradually increase the distance as you explore your community on foot before going on your first backpack. Christmas boots would be well broken in for the spring and summer hiking season. Unfortunately, many boot stores do not stock up until spring.

I hope you've gotten the impression that boots and socks are important, because they most definitely are!

Hiking
Clothing

Essential Clothing

The volume and weight of equipment decreases by necessity as the vacationer makes the change from cottages, trailers, car camping, or canoe camping to backpacking. It stands to reason that in backpacking each and every item carried must be considered on an "essential" basis, rather than a "nice-to-have" basis. So it is with each item of clothing.

Socks

We have previously established that you'll be wearing one pair of boots and one pair of socks, plus carrying one spare pair of socks in your pack. You may alternate socks and spare socks each day, or whatever system suits your mood; as long as your socks are dry there is no functional reason to change them. As a practical matter most hikers will change into a dry pair of socks each day; I prefer to change each night before bed, as this provides me with warm dry feet all through the night.

Underwear

Undershorts should be a little loose, rather than a little snug. Tiny irritations have a way of magnifying on a long hike. Wear one pair and carry one spare pair. Nylon undershorts dry quickly after rinsing; cotton dries slowly. Some men favor an undershirt. If you do wear an undershirt, consider a cotton T-shirt, as it not only serves as a lightweight shirt for hot days, but will also provide material for compresses, bandages and slings, should the occasion for their use arise. Potential multifunctional items make a lot of sense in backpacking when you are one, two, three or more days away from assistance.

T-shirts cover the shoulders and reduce friction from pack shoulder straps and also offer protection from sunburn. If you happen to sunburn your shoulders on a backpack you may end up carrying your pack on your head, as one of my scouts did on a 3½-mile hike. Being somewhat leary of sunburned shoulders, I rarely take off my T-shirt.

Long Trousers and Hiking Shorts

Roomy trousers, such as workmen's full-cut jeans, are preferable to snug trousers. You'll literally take thousands of steps and each might as well be as friction free as possible. New jeans should be washed and worn a few times to soften them before hiking. Jeans protect your legs from scratches, insects, and sunburn. They dry quickly when wet and their tight weave resists snags. Colors available are red, russet, green, tan, and the familiar blue jeans. White is depressing when dirty. One pair of jeans is worn, with no spares carried. If you must wear hiking shorts, take a lightweight nylon pair to wear in camp, but hike in long jeans. Beware of sunburned thighs. If by religious conviction you are a sunworshipper, like Connie, disregard this advice entirely.

For cool spring and fall hiking I once was able to buy three pairs of tightly woven, hard-finished wool uniform trousers at a church rummage sale for 50¢ a pair. The worst pair was cannibalized, the material used for reinforced seats and knees on the other two pairs. Cargo pockets were added. The result was two pairs of excellent cool-weather hiking-climbing trousers that have served me well for six years so far.

Long-Sleeved Shirt

Wear or pack one long- or short-sleeved shirt; long sleeves if insects are known to be in your hiking area, and short sleeves if not. Tightly woven fabrics such as a pima cotton workshirt (65% polyester and 35% cotton) resist wind and are preferable to loose weaves, as they do not snag.

We have now discussed two layers of clothing: (1) undershirt; (2) workshirt. Wear one or both according to the temperature and wind velocity. If you wear one you obviously need room to pack the other.

Multipurpose Clothing

Backpacks of a week or longer may start in sunshine, change to cool, cloudy days, and on the week selected for your vacation may deteriorate into a chilling rain. Hiking through mountain passes will generally be windy, almost always chilly, and sometimes cold. You may count on the unpredictability of mountain weather. Even if the weather is perfect, you can usually count on the fact that full sun is hot, shadows chilling, and nights cool, or occasionally cold (35 degrees). To carry clothing for all those variables, a few garments must serve multiple functions and do it with low weight and little volume, since pack space is limited.

Long-Sleeved Sweater

For clothing layer (3), a long-sleeved, tight-knit, lightweight Orlon sweater is nearly perfect. Long sleeves are necessary as nylon down jackets or nylon rain jackets feel cold as ice against bare skin. They feel warmer when worn over a long-sleeved sweater. Shop for irregulars, or sweaters on sale; you don't need an expensive, first-class, high-fashion model. Avoid turtlenecks or mock turtlenecks as they tend to irritate your neck after a day or two. Many excellent sweaters are available at rummage sales for a fraction of their original cost. If you feel cold and clammy, Orlon next to your body is warm, but not scratchy. If you sweat a lot, and as a consequence feel chilly, Orlon next to your body is almost essential, since it is warm even when wet. Cotton fabrics such as net underwear are cold as ice when wet from sweat and should be avoided. Why doesn't some intelligent manufacturer produce Orlon net undershirts? An Orlon sweater is also an excellent pajama top; warm, soft, and does not absorb body-water vapor given off while you sleep. Jazzy designs and colors help your morale and provide a conversation piece for your fellow hikers.

Down Jacket

For clothing layer (4), nothing, absolutely nothing, beats a goose down-filled, long-sleeved, lightweight nylon jacket. Lightest weight and lowest cost down-filled nylon jacket turns out to be a down undershirt. Don't let the name throw you; be objective. A down undershirt looks and functions exactly the same as an expensive down jacket; it merely cost less and weighs less. Most have knitted nylon cuffs, some have knitted nylon collars, while others have nylon mandarin collars. Snaps are preferable to zippers, as the overall weight is less. Goose-down undershirts (hereafter called "jackets") compress into a small volume, weigh 15 to 16 total ounces, and cost about $25. Down nylon jackets worn directly against your bare skin feel cold, so I would suggest wearing your jacket over a long-sleeved shirt (layer 2), or preferably *over your long-sleeved Orlon sweater* (layer 3). As a matter of temperature reference, a down jacket (16 total ounces) over an Orlon long-sleeve sweater (next to my body) will keep me comfortable at 35 degrees above zero with little or no wind. Test out your own temperature tolerance so that you have confidence in the clothing you are backpacking. Goose-down jackets may be handwashed at home and air or machine dried on a cool setting, or, dried in sunshine. Fluff up when dry to restore the insulation value.

Windbreaker Jacket

A combination windbreaker-rain jacket is essential to reduce loss of body heat from wind and constitutes layer (5). Coated nylon fabrics that "breathe" or are vented weigh about 10 ounces and cost as little as $12. Drawstring hoods (essential) are tucked into a zippered mandarin collar. Rain jacket may be worn over any or all layers of clothing, either during a rain, *or, more frequently,* as a windbreaker during high wind. A coated nylon rain jacket worn directly next to the bare skin feels cold and is more comfortable worn over a long-sleeved shirt, or preferably over a *long-sleeved Orlon sweater.* I prefer an orange-colored rain jacket, as it is highly visible in bad weather. Orange is the international distress color and can come in handy for signaling for help, should the occasion arise. Might as well combine as many functions as possible into your clothing, particularly when color does not increase weight or volume.

Clothing Temperature Range

With the (5) layers of clothing described *most summer mountain temperatures are comfortably handled during daylight hours in the 6,000 to 11,000 foot* altitude range.

Please note that additional layers of clothing are put on at the *first sign* of a chill. Clothing put on *before you are chilled* throughout is effective; if clothing is put on *after you are chilled,* it takes forever to become warm again. You'll get no medals for quietly shivering. If you develop the sniffles, you will learn how welcome a cougher or sneezer is inside a tiny two-person mountain tent.

You can visualize the various combinations of body insulation provided by the five layers of clothing. These may be modified slightly to taste, but the essential items are:

(1) T-shirt
(2) shirt to avoid insects and sunburned shoulders
(3) *long-sleeved* Orlon sweater
(4) goose-down jacket
(5) nylon windbreaker-rain jacket *with hood*

Layers of clothing provide choice for the many different temperatures encountered on a mountain backpack. Layers of clothing weigh less than a single heavy garment, and are warmer because air gets trapped between the layers.

Bandana

To keep sweat out of your eyes, and to hold your hair in place, a *large* red bandana will complete your wardrobe. It doubles as a hat, hot-pot holder, washrag, mop, bandage and sling. Generally your red bandana will become rather grayish by the time you reach the trail's end.

Try Out Boots and Clothing

There is merit in trying out your new boots and various clothing combinations on one-day hikes to local parks where you can also practice cooking a simple one-pot meal at lunchtime. By getting used to wearing hiking boots and hiking clothes you will build up your confidence in your clothing, as well as slowly increasing your hiking mileage to picturesque lunchsites. Spare clothing, pots, cups, and food may be carried in an inexpensive small pack known as a "day pack," a fun pack to own which will come in handy on backpacks when you wish to take a one-day hike from your base camp. Skiers use day packs to transport elegant lunches to high, sheltered, sunny places where food and sun are enjoyed. Your hike to a local park with a welcome picnic luncheon is also an excellent way to introduce your spouse and children to hiking and picnics. Too much too soon and they'll turn off; one step at a time and they'll look forward to the next outing. Don't forget the first-aid bag.

Spare clothing is carried in lightweight, waterproof plastic bags for protection from rain, evening dampness, spilled water bottles, etc. You might begin saving *unperforated* plastic bags, such as bread bags, bags inside salted-cracker boxes, ice-cream bags, and fresh-vegetable bags (best), as they can be used for first-aid bags, food bags, etc. You'll need about 75% small individual food bags and 25% larger bags for entire meals.

Briefly, your backpacking clothing for a two-day to two-week summer hike may be summarized as follows:

Wear	Carry in Plastic Bag in Pack
1 pair hiking boots	1 pair ski socks or hiking socks
1 pair ski socks or hiking socks	1 pair undershorts
1 pair undershorts	1 T-shirt (optional)
1 T-shirt (optional)	1 long-sleeved Orlon sweater (6 oz.)
1 long- or short-sleeved shirt	*1 down-filled nylon jacket (16 oz.)
1 bandana	**1 rain jacket with hood (10 oz.)
	**1 pair hiking shorts (optional)

*Inside separate plastic bag in pack pocket.
**Easily accessible in pack pocket or top of pack.

Sleeping Bags and Foam Pads

Weight and Volume Criteria

Like all items carried, sleeping-bag weight and rolled-up compressed volume partially determine the difference between a backpack and a burden. Total sleeping-bag weight of about four pounds, preferably less, is desirable. Compressed volume will measure six to eight inches diameter by one-half of the sleeping-bag width.

If your existing sleeping bag approximately fits the above criteria, you're in; if it's heavier or bigger in diameter, you may wish to give your old sleeping bag to one of your nonbackpacking children and acquire a new lighter weight sleeping bag. Assuming you are starting from scratch, below are some of the qualities of a reasonable backpacking *mummy sleeping bag used inside a tent for summer temperatures down to about 35 degrees, plus or minus five degrees:*

Dacron Filled	*Down Filled*
Total Weight 4¼ lbs.	3 lb. 4 oz. to 3 lb. 10 oz.
Filling Weight 3 lbs.	1½ to 2 lbs.

Heavier Insulation

Avoid the temptation to buy heavier filling weights of Dacron or goose down, as they are too hot, e.g., a two-pound goose down-filled bag doesn't begin to feel comfortable to me until temperature drops to 35 degrees. Of course that's my metabolism, not yours, but it does provide you with at least a yardstick by which to gauge comfort. It would be ideal if suppliers sold sleeping bags with disposable paper liners, so that the buying public could actually try out the comfort range under controlled conditions in their own homes. Then a too-hot or too-cold bag could be exchanged (unsoiled) for a proper comfort-range bag. Paper liners would also permit buyers to determine if a bag were too short or too long, or if a bag had sufficient girth or not enough.

Fabric and Zippers

Inner lining and outer cover should be tough, light-weight, *untreated* nylon known as "ripstop" nylon. Slippery nylon inner lining permits your clothed body to move within the bag; cotton linings prevent movement, hold body-water vapor and are heavier than nylon. You can't afford the additional weight or clutter of separate snap-in inner linings or outer wind-shells, so forget it. Bags are not waterproof nor water resistant, nor should they be, as your body-water vapors *must escape from the bag*. If water vapors do not escape, the Dacron or goose down-insulation becomes damp, and the insulation value is *immediately reduced*. In other words, you are in trouble.

Bags without zippers weigh less but require squirming and wiggling to enter and exit and may be too hot in the early evening hours, since they may not be opened by unzipping. Zippers of about 36 inches in length permit easy entry and exit, and may be partially opened on warm nights. Full-length zippers permit paired matching bags, but weigh more than bags with 36-inch zippers; however, there are compensations. On the inside of the bag, right behind the zipper opening, manufacturers place an insulation-filled tube, which runs the full length of the zipper, to prevent body heat from escaping through the zipper teeth.

Steel zippers seem to jam more than aluminum or nylon zippers. Tiny-toothed zippers jam easier than medium- to large-toothed zippers. Pull-tabs to open the zipper should be both inside and outside the bag. When you lose a pull-tab you can improvise (at home) by drilling a tiny hole through where the tab formerly fastened, inserting a paper clip, and covering the paper clip with adhesive tape. One such modification on my bag has functioned well for four years.

An excellent way to avoid jamming the fabric in the zipper is to keep both sides of the zipper parallel and close together just ahead of the area being zipped. Also, keep one finger inside, between the insulated tube and zipper, to keep the insulated tube and inner-lining fabric out of the way of the locking teeth. If a zipper jams shut you're warm; if it jams open you're in trouble. Your only alternatives are to pin the zipper closed, sew it closed, or simply roll over with the opened zipper facing down and sleep on your stomach on top of your foam mattress pad.

Bag Length and Shape

Bags are available in lengths for average and tall people. Shorter people have an economic advantage as less expensive children's-size bags *may* fit them perfectly.

Sleeping-bag shape is extremely important for warmth, weight and volume considerations. Body warmth inside a sleeping bag is almost like body warmth inside a home. Food is comparable to furnace fuel. Your body converts food to body heat just as a furnace converts fuel to heat. Larger space inside a rectangular-shaped bag requires more heated air than a smaller space inside a mummy bag. Big rooms require more heated air than smaller rooms. More space inside the bag induces drafts since there is more air available; less space inside the bag reduces drafts since there is less air available. Draft-free bags and rooms seem warmer than drafty bags and drafty rooms. Insulated walls of the bag retain heat as do insulated walls of a house.

Water vapor reduces insulation value and must

either be kept out of a house wall or allowed to pass through; human body-produced water vapor cannot be kept out of a bag, hence it must be allowed to pass through the bag. Do not buy sleeping bags advertised as waterproof or water resistant, as they will retain body-water vapor and reduce insulation value of the bag.

Wind robs heat. Sheltered homes and bags sheltered inside tents are decidedly warmer; two authorities say they are ten to twenty degrees warmer. I can accept about five degrees to 10 degrees warmer, but I'd want to record inside and outside temperatures over a period of time before advocating a differential of as much as 20 degrees.

Body warmth is related to all of the above and in particular to insulation thickness. For the same total weight of bag and insulation, more insulation thickness is possible in a mummy bag than in a rectangular bag, as there is less surface area in a mummy bag. Two areas of your body are especially sensitive to feeling warm or cold: your feet (wear dry socks to bed), and your head. Mummy bags keep your head warm, which is critical.

Mummy Bags vs Rectangular Bags

Mummy bags, although their filling weight is equal to that of rectangular bags, are generally lighter in overall weight as they require less lining, less zipper, less stitching and less cover material. Mummy bags occupy less floor space inside a tapered mountain tent and compress to less volume inside a pack than rectangular bags do. These are important considerations.

So far, in our family of eight, five of us have converted to mummy bags, with three holdouts. Since all of us were brought up on rectangular bags, there is a certain psychological block to improving things by moving into a mummy bag, which appears smaller (remember that to some people bigger is better); however, once the switch has been accomplished, the better performance of a mummy bag is greatly appreciated.

No mummy-bag user in our family ever expressed an interest in switching back to a rectangular bag.

What it boils down to is this: in a rectangular bag your body turns within the bag; in a mummy bag you and the bag turn together. In other words, you *wear* a mummy bag. Once that concept has seeped into your subconscious, you accept it as logically as you accept wearing a hooded jacket.

If you are a holdout, please wear a ski hat when you go to bed, and consider buying a warmer bag—you'll probably need it!

Insulated Inner Bags

If your hiking partner is a talented sewer, she could make a one- or two-pound Dacron-filled nylon bag to serve as an inner bag to fit inside your three-pound Dacron bag so that its use can be extended into cooler spring and fall weather. I have such a liner, but only used it once as it takes up too much space inside the pack. In spring or fall I wear more clothing inside my mummy bag and leave the liner at home.

For winter camping our family has used two three-pound Dacron mummy bags, one nested inside the other. We each wear dry ski socks, cotton-wool long johns, Dacron-insulated underwear trousers, two Orlon sweaters, a down jacket and a wool ski hat. Good for at least 12 degrees below zero inside a tent after an energy-packed supper. Experiment for cold-temperature camping in your backyard; that's what we did before going on winter camps. If something went wrong, we could always come into the house and correct the problem.

Down Bag For Summer

I rarely use my two-pound goose down-filled bag, as it is too hot for comfort in summer mountain weather. For me a 1½- to 1¾-pound down-filled bag with an overall weight of 2¾ pounds would seem ideal. I'd also like to buy it for about $35 to $45; however, I haven't seen any offered at that price. Mentally, manufacturers are high altitude, expedition conscious, which is excellent and beneficial to the persons engaged in those pursuits. However, the bulk of backpackers are not in that category, even if they imagine themselves to be. A low-cost, high-class, lightweight mummy sleeping bag of goose or duck down would be appreciated by multitudes of summer backpackers. Such a bag could also serve as a liner for other down bags for a manufacturer who realized the value of an integrated line of mummy bags. For example, Mom and Dad could each summer backpack in one bag apiece, while Dad could spring and fall backpack "with the boys" by nesting one bag inside the other.

Dacron vs Down Insulation

There are certain pros and cons on Dacron vs Down which we ought to explore. One of the big ones is a rain-soaked sleeping bag. Dacron can be successfully dried near a campfire; however, don't hold it too close, as high heat tends to matt Dacron. Down is almost impossible to dry out, *and a wet or damp down bag is a serious problem.* Down is excellent in a dry environment or in a cold environment where rain doesn't happen (e.g., winter camping, or high-altitude camping).

The best way, of course, to avoid wet-bag crises is to keep your sleeping bag dry. Pack it inside a plastic bag if your sleeping bag is carried inside your pack, or, pack it in a plastic bag inside a waterproof stuff sack if your bag is carried outside your pack.

If you sleep on your side, as I do, the down insulation may tend to shift from under your body to above your body, which is great, right up to the moment you roll over on the other side and freeze. I eagerly took my down bag on one first and last hike. I know there are better-built down bags than mine that are designed to prevent the down from shifting from bottom to top. Catalog illustrations refer to a baffle running along the length of the bag, designed to keep "top" and "bottom" down fillings from visiting one another. My Dacron bag may be low cost, but its uniform thickness is also dependable, top or bottom.

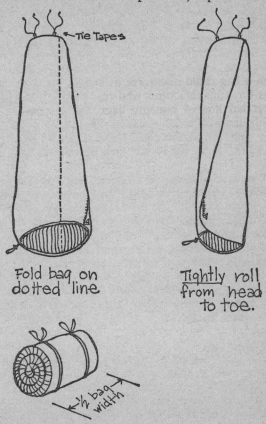

Fold bag on dotted line

Tightly roll from head to toe.

Compressing Bag

To roll a bag, zip it closed, fold it to one-half width, then begin at the head end and roll toward the foot while simultaneously pressing down with your hands to compress the bag. Tie with tapes sewn into the foot of the bag. We replaced tie strings, which cut into fingers, with cotton tie tapes, or tough, flat cotton shoe laces that do not cut into fingers. Manufacturers please note: our modified tie tape extends inside the foot of the bag as a small one-inch loop so that nesting bags may be joined together with tie tapes through loops.

Keep Mummy Bag Dry

Your mummy bag may get wet or damp, even though inside your tent, from any one or a combination of the following causes:

1. Exhaling inside your bag. Keep your nose outside your bag.

2. Placing waterproof rainwear over your bag in an attempt to become warmer. Body-water vapor cannot get through the rainwear and will condense on the underside of the rainwear and rub or drip on your bag.

3. Condensation on the inside tent walls may rub or drip on your bag.

4. Rubbing against a cotton-tent sidewall or roof during a rain may break the water membrane across the tiny openings between threads and may induce a slow leak.

5. Spilling food or drink on your bag.

Causes 1, 2, 3, 4, and 5 are all under your control.

Cleaning and Repairing Bags

When home from the hills, turn your bag inside out and dry it thoroughly in the sun and air, or dry it for one or two days indoors. Store your bag folded loosely; do not leave it compressed and rolled up, as the thickness tends to diminish over time. We have retired bags, but have never totally washed or dry cleaned a bag. Bags cost money and I don't plan to harm any stitching, fabrics or insulation. Any spots are honest and certainly don't hurt anyone.

Rips may be repaired temporarily in the field with ripstop nylon tape until permanently repaired by sewing on patches cut in happy shapes, with stitched designs, or with the owner's name or initials on the patch. Patches stuck on with a hot iron are quick, but might be hazardous if the fabric melts in high heat. Loose or missing stitching should be replaced. Test proposed spot removers first on a tiny noncritical area, as some spot removers, such as lacquer thinner, may dissolve nylon. Turpentine is friendlier and responds well to its drippy cousin, pine resin.

Bedrolls and Mattresses

When our family first began backpacking we couldn't afford sleeping bags, so we used interfolded blankets secured with blanket pins to form a bedroll. These bedrolls were wrapped in vinyl to keep out the rain, and draped horseshoe-style over the top and sides of our pack in the manner of a World War I doughboy. We still say "bedroll" when we mean "sleeping bag."

Not only did we not have sleeping bags, but we didn't know about, or at least didn't own, mattresses of any kind. Outer clothing was placed under our bedrolls to insulate our bodies from ground cold. We used this system down to 28 degrees. This is the logic of the sleeping-naked myth, which goes back to prefoam pad days and down-filled bags. Obviously, some type of insulation was needed under the down bags, as down compresses and its insulation value is lost; clothes were available, hence clothes were used. In turn, down bags had to be warmer to compensate for the nude sleeper. To advocates of nude sleeping: try going to the john on a winter night; it will either kill you or cure you.

Eventually we located and bought heavy 2¾-pound surplus GI air mattresses which squished and squeaked with every turn and were not as warm as placing our clothing under our bedrolls. When air mattresses performed as intended, they cushioned and cradled my tired body; it felt somewhat like being in a ship gently rocking at anchor.

Being a creature of the land more than the sea, I never became used to the swishing and swaying that occurred with each turn.

Lighter Weight Foam Pads

Our transition to foam mattress pads occurred on a car camp when we used a covered foam pad borrowed from a bench in our living room. Comfort and insulation from ground cold were immediately apparent. It was a short mental hike to the uncovered, lower weight, urethane foam pads that we now use.

We have experimented with various thicknesses (¼ inch, ¾ inch, 1 inch, and 1½ inches) and various lengths (short, medium and body length) of foam

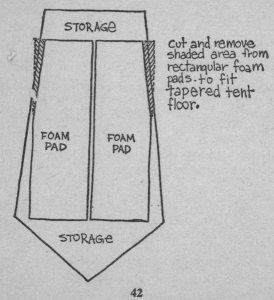

STORAGE

Cut and remove shaded area from rectangular foam pads to fit tapered tent floor.

FOAM PAD

FOAM PAD

STORAGE

pads, and have finally standardized on 1½-inch thick, 20-inch wide, body-length urethane foam pads, which can be cut with scissors to fit the tapered floor plan of a two-person mountain tent. Uncovered pads cost less, weigh less, and have less volume than covered pads, hence they are suitable for backpacking.

Foam pads are compressed with hands and knee and rolled into a cylindrical shape and further compressed with a 15-foot length of ⅛-inch thick nylon line wrapped tightly around the pad. Rolled compressed pads (three to four inches diameter) may be placed on the top of packs under the flap, or after folding to proper size and rolling, they may be placed inside your pack on short backpacks when you do not need pack volume for food bags. Try out your foam pads and mummy bags in your home, patio, deck or lawn, or on your next car camp and *get used to them* prior to your first backpack.

Low Total Cost

Son Tom has requested that I point out that expensive equipment is not a requirement of backpacking. Quite the contrary, equipment is meager and therefore backpacking *total costs are low*. Specifically, quality mummy bags are available with three pounds of Dacron filling, ripstop-nylon lining and cover, and medium-toothed nylon zippers that weigh 4¼ pounds overall, and which are suitable for 99% of summer backpacking. On those occasions when the weather is a bit cool, simply put on your Orlon sweater, or if you are still cool, put on your down jacket over your Orlon sweater. Cost of a three-pound Dacron-filled mummy bag is about $25 in the Seattle area.

More people have associated summer backpacking with $100 down bags. The myth isn't valid. Few people need down in summer, and fewer people backpack in winter.

A $25 Dacron mummy bag used inside a vented tent is just as warm as a $100 down mummy bag used in the open, and a $100 down mummy bag used inside a tent may be too warm. The chief advantage of owning a down bag is low weight and low volume. Both are highly desirable features.

Backpacking Tents

Common Tent Features

Mountain tents come in a multitude of prices, colors, shapes and sizes, but generally they have certain common features:

Designed for two hikers and their gear
Tent-pole-pin total weight: five to seven pounds
Roll to size of loaf of bread
Low profile to reduce wind load
Waterproof floor
Mosquito netting
Zippered door or tunnel

On routes where trees or *sturdy* fallen branches *are certain,* you may wish to eliminate the one pound of tent poles and substitute a 50-foot coil of ⅛-inch thick nylon line to rig your poleless tent. The tent may pitch a little droopy, but you'll droop a little less as one pound has been eliminated from your pack load. You can almost always eliminate the rear poles if you have a packframe or ice axe. Both ideas are worth serious consideration.

Waterproof Tent Floors

Tents should have coated nylon waterproof floors so that ground dampness does not come up and attack you. If the floor is not waterproof, then place a cut-to-size sheet of vinyl between tent floor and ground. Plastic should be cut undersize in all dimensions so that it does not hang out and unwittingly collect water from rain and conduct it under and into your tent. One book on backpacking repeats this error in several illustrations of pitched tents. If your tent doesn't have any floor, then place the vinyl ground cloth on the ground under your foam pads. If you don't have a tent, read on and you will be able to discriminate between types available.

Several basic fabrics are used in two-person tents. Some are "old-fashioned" and others are "modern." Some "old" is both good and bad; some "modern" is both good and bad.

Untreated Cotton Tents

Tightly woven untreated cotton, repeat *untreated,* with a thread count of 200 threads per lineal inch, is an excellent fabric. I am *not* referring to treated cotton drill, which is a heavy, poor fabric not suited to backpacking. When untreated cotton is first wetted in a rain, the impact of the raindrops may cause a fine "mist" inside the tent that persists for a few seconds until the thread fibers absorb water and swell, reducing the opening size between threads, similar to cedarwood shingles swelling in a rain. Rainwater bridges the tiny openings between swollen threads and further "misting" will not occur. I'm not sure I can remember if our cotton tent ever "misted" or not. My convertible car roof is pure untreated cotton and has yet to "mist" or leak one drop.

Cotton tents are excellent and will not leak under high wind and rain, as long as the roof or side walls are not touched. Touching theoretically breaks the delicate water membrane bridging the tiny openings between threads, and may induce a slow leak, but not always. Knowing this fact, you are not going to poke your fingers into a roof during a rain, at least not on my side of the tent. Our family has happily camped in untreated cotton tents for 13 years and has found them to be rainproof and windproof; but don't touch roof or sidewalls during a rain, as they may leak.

The cotton single-wall tent transmits sun heat effectively inside the tent, a welcome feature on cold mornings in the mountains. Cotton "breathes" and transmits body-water vapors and cooking-water vapors outside through the tent walls. Water vapor will not condense and collect on the inside of a cotton tent unless it is iced on the outside, in which case inside vapor takes on the physical form of frost, which evaporates as sun heat strikes the tent, or stays put if the sun doesn't shine.

Most cotton two-person tents are made in "pup tent" styles by Eastern and Southern manufacturers. Pup tents are wider and higher at the foot than tapered "mountain tents" and as a result generally weigh more than mountain tents. If cotton tents were available in tapered width and tapered height, then fabric, stitching, seams, and rear tent pole weight would decrease by about one pound.

Total weight of quality cotton two-person pup tents varies from 7½ to 10½ pounds, including poles and pins. While weight is up, cost is down to $30 to $60.

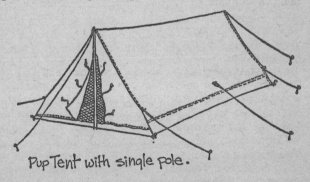

Pup Tent with single pole.

Pima Cloth Tents

Cotton pima cloth (polyester and cotton blend) is another excellent tent fabric subject to the same finger-poking precautions as a cotton tent. The higher the thread count per lineal inch the better; the cotton thread does all the work of swelling and closing openings between threads, since the polyester does not absorb water. We have three two-person pima cloth tents in our family and they have provided excellent service in the driving rains of Europe, the Midwest, and the drizzles of the Pacific Northwest for over six years. One tent cost $37 in 1967, and two others were eagerly bought on sale for $26 apiece. Pima cloth tents may "mist" for a few seconds at the beginning of rain, as cotton tents do. I can only recall one "misting," in Wisconsin, that was over before it started. The misting stops as soon as the cotton threads swell. Rain will seep through stitching at the sidewall-floor junction. Seam sealers are available and may or may not cure the problem. Worth trying.

Being single walled, a pima cloth tent admits sun heat into your tent on a cold morning. Pima cloth "breathes," permitting body-water vapors and cooking vapors to escape to the cold outer air. Condensation will not occur on the inside unless the outside is covered with ice, in which case the inside will be frost-covered, not wet.

If you are fortunate enough to locate a pima cloth tent, buy it quickly. Most manufacturers have abandoned making this rugged, inexpensive tent in favor of models costing two and three times as much. I understand the manufacturer's monetary needs, but does he understand mine?

Pima cloth two-person mountain tents weigh about 5½ to 6 pounds, including poles and pins. Weight and costs are less than cotton. Price range was about $40 for a medium-quality tent; however, they are now apparently extinct.

Untreated Nylon Plus Coated Nylon Fly

Untreated nylon tent fabric sheds wind and is fine for dry or cold weather, or both, but it is quickly penetrated by rain. If untreated nylon is used in wet regions, it must be covered with a waterproof covering known as a "tent fly," which is generally made from coated nylon fabric. Wind-driven rain gets under the coated tent fly and wets the lower portions of tent sidewalls. For this reason, and to repell snow dampness, lower tent sidewalls are usually extensions of the same waterproof material used in tent floors, or at least they ought to be. With the turned up floor-sidewall the fly is effective, except at front-door openings, where most flys do not cover the opening; hence the zippered flap allows rain to leak in (as do most zippered flaps). Sidewall-floor junction seams will leak, as it does in a pima cotton tent. Some models have the waterproof floor turn up about six to eight inches, which cures the problem.

Tent flys prevent water from penetrating the tent; they also prevent sun heat from penetrating the tent on a cold morning, as the fly casts a shadow on the inner tent. This is great for hot climates but poor for cold ones. Since tent flys are by definition waterproof, the water vapor from body or cooking passes through the inner untreated tent nylon and escapes onto the inner face of the exterior coated-nylon fly. Vapor will condense and in a wind-driven rain the poorly guyed fly will press against the inner tent, wet the inner-tent fabric and hence may dampen sleeping bags. True, some vapor will escape between tent and tent fly, but not all. The closer the fly is located to the inner tent the higher the probability of condensation and resultant inner-tent wetting.

Manufacturers please note: tents with flys droop inside; as the inner tent is not guyed out. Neither are flys guyed out at sidewall centers. If fly were guyed out, and a short loop connected fly to tent, then a guyed fly would also guy out the inner-tent sidewall.

In time, coated flys lose their waterproof characteristics and must be replaced. While untreated nylon tents (without coated fly) weigh less than cotton or pima cloth tents, the combined weight of untreated nylon tent and coated nylon fly is a little more or a little less than pima cloth tents. One gorgeous untreated nylon tent and coated fly, the identical total weight of my pima cloth tent, costs about 3½ times as much. Space, style, etc. are equal. The waterproof floor turns up about six inches, which is an advantage lacking in my tent.

Weight of untreated nylon tents with coated nylon fly, poles and pins range from 5⅛ pounds for two-person mountain tents, up to 8¼ pounds for pup-tent models, not including expedition models, which are even heavier. Costs of untreated nylon tents with coated nylon flys range from $78 to $140.

If I had any one suggestion for manufacturers of this type of tent, it would be to fit the fly far better than is presently done and to guy it in such a way that it will not press into the inner tent and thus negate the major *raison d'etre* of a tent fly.

Coated Nylon Tents

Coated nylon tents weigh less than any other tents and are logically designed with various vents to allow the water vapor from body or cooking to pass out through the vents.

Now, water vapor is not overly bright and while it may really want to escape through the vents, a lot of it doesn't make it and bumps into the coated tent sidewalls. Since tent sidewalls resist the passage of water vapor and are as cold or colder than the dew point, the vapor condenses on the inside of the tent where it is free to drip or rub off on your mummy bag. World War II mountain troops suffered in these sweat boxes, although admittedly they were not vented. As soon as water vapor can be better trained to exit through the vents these coated tents will become practical. Sidewall-floor junctions leak through the stitching, as other tents do.

Eventually, as the coating wears off, more water vapor escapes, but more rainwater penetrates. Coated nylon tents weigh about 4½ pounds, including poles and pins. Cost ranges from $25 to $40.

Selecting a Tent

As a guide to selecting a tent, a few factors to consider are: initial cost, windproof, usable space, escape of water vapor, repairability, sun heat, color, rolled compressed volume, overall weight including poles and pins, low or high profile, and availability.

At present your choice boils down to:

(1) untreated cotton

(2) untreated nylon with coated nylon fly

(3) coated nylon, which will produce condensation problems

Low and High Profile Tents

Low-profile tents are tapered in height from front to rear and offer less resistance to wind, which can whip a tent to shreds. The best low-profile tents are also tapered in width from front to rear, which fits a rear

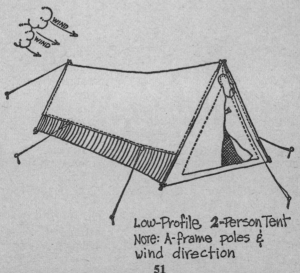

Low-Profile 2-Person Tent
NOTE: A-frame poles &
wind direction

wind quite well. A pup tent with horizontal roof lines is an example of a high-profile tent. While a pup tent offers more interior volume, it does not offer more *usable* interior space.

Tapering of both rear height and width reduces tent weight because material, seams, stitching and rear tent-pole height are all reduced. Generally, low-profile tents weigh less than pup-tent styles made of the same materials.

Vestibule

Storage for packs and cooking inside a tent are simplified by a triangular floor space in front of the tent, known as a "vestibule." Another method of providing storage and cooking space is to make a tent longer. The vestibule method weighs less than the longer-tent method. Vestibule should be floored, and in some tents it has a zippered floor opening known as a "cooking hole" for disposing of excess food.

Tent Poles

"A-shaped" front tent poles help maintain the width of the tent in a wind or windy rain and facilitate getting in and out, as poles are not in the center of the door opening. "A-shaped" poles are really two poles, one on each side of the tent, which weigh more than one tent pole planted in the middle of the door opening, but at least enable you to get in and out of the tent easily.

Regardless of pole style, the poles ought at least to be sectionalized so that disassembled pole height is reduced; preferably they should be telescoped so that sections fit inside one another. Telescoping poles take the least volume in a pack. They also jam or bind quite easily if bent or allowed to pick up dirt, which gouges pole surface and thereby slightly enlarges the diameter, thus ruining a good fit. Usually one pole section will push out a reluctant section, or a tent pin may be used to prod the stubborn pole into action.

To protect poles from dust and injurious grit, carry poles in a cloth pole bag. Poles are kept together and the chance of them falling out of a pack is minimized. Cloth for my tent-pole was a 10¢ fabric sample. The bag has a flap to cover ends of poles and tie tapes to secure the flap. I slide the pole bag down inside a corner of my pack, flap side down, so poles won't jump out along the trail.

Tent Pins

Tent pins that come with most tents are rather pathetic and are generally too heavy, too thick, too short, or a combination. Happily, lightweight, strong, thin, hard aluminum wire pins are manufactured in England and are available in the United States in nine- and ten-inch lengths, which despite severe wind or rainstorm hold well in most soils, excluding sand or snow. Pins are about ⅛-inch in diameter and have a loop on one end. Pins will stray about unless confined in a simple cloth bag with tie tapes.

Tent Guylines

Tent ropes and wood or metal slides (guyline tighteners) furnished with most tents are also rather sad. Ropes may be used for a household clothes line, as most are too heavy and bulky to be used in backpacking. Most practical tent lines are ⅛-inch nylon; thinner lines are adequate but difficult to tie for stubby or cold fingers. Lines may be obtained in white or red. If your tent does not come with nylon guylines, you'd be well advised to buy and install them before your first backpack. To give you some idea of guyline length for ordering purposes, the following is suggested for a low-profile tent:

Front—8 feet

Side—6 feet

Back—4 feet (use 8 feet for a high-profile tent)

Longer lines are more useful (up to a point) than shorter lines. Burn each cut end of your nylon tent lines with a lighted match to keep ends from fraying. Hot melted nylon burns severely, so use caution. Lines are attached to tent loops with a tiny bowline knot, which you will learn to tie later on in this book.

You don't need wood or metal slides. You'll be using a secure sliding knot, known as a "tautline," which is a more versatile means of tightening guylines in situations where a metal slide would be useless, such as guying to a shrub or branch. Slides get lost; the knowledge of how to tie a knot does not.

Tent Modification

Tents should be pitched taut to resist flapping to shreds in the inevitable high winds of nighttime. Our two-person tent was a little floppy in the front sides, no matter how the tent was rigged. Lying in the tent one morning and contemplating the floppy sidewalls, I began pushing out on the tent sidewalls at various locations until one spot seemed to make the entire side taut. Connie did the same on the other side of the tent and magically our tent became tauter and roomier. We noted the locations and when back home Connie sewed 4-inch by 4-inch reinforcing patches *inside* the tent and sewed 2-inch by 2-inch reinforcing patches on the *outside* of the tent centered over the inside patches. Half-inch-wide nylon loops, with burned ends to prevent fraying, were centered and sewn to the 2-inch by 2-inch patch, sewing through both inside and outside patches to distribute the strain to the tent sidewalls.

This modification has made our tent very solid in high winds. Material for the patches came from a tent bag of the same color and material as the tent. I suppose this is another good argument for cotton or pima cloth tents; namely, they can be repaired and modified at home on a regular sewing machine with little or no cash expenditure and without knowledge of plastics technology. So many "improvements" seem to prevent man from repairing or modifying his own property.

Our original pima cloth two-person mountain tent was given to our oldest son, Chuck, who used it in Greece, Israel, Turkey, Italy, France and Switzerland. Chuck said the tent never leaked, although water entered through the front zippered door flap during a severe rainstorm in Switzerland. Other than a small hole in the floor, it is in excellent condition. His tent was modified with an overhead nylon line running from the tent's high point to the tent's mid point. The line is 1/16-inch nylon, hand-stitched to the tent roof seam at several points. Handy for hanging up eyeglasses, damp socks, or for suspending a tiny flashlight to facilitate midnight reading or snacking.

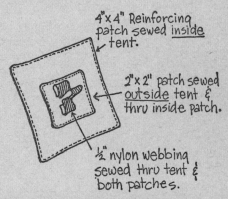

TENT REINFORCING PATCH

Pitching a Tent

To locate a tent on the flat spot or knoll you have selected, point the rear of the tent uphill facing the mountains. This does not mean your tent is sloping— your tent is level—but the rear faces uphill. Air becomes cooler at night and the heavier cool air falls

downhill, creating winds better resisted by the low profile and tapered rear end of a tent. Less flapping will
result than if pitched with sides pointing uphill. Front-
to-the-wind invites wind-driven rain to penetrate the
front zipper on the door flaps. Obviously the desired
orientation is not always possible.

Pin the rear of the tent to the ground then pull snugly to the front and pin the front. Finally, pin each side
to the ground. When using aluminum wire pins with
loops on the end, the tent loop slips off the pin and
goes $3/8$-inch inside the pin loop; thus, a tight fit ends
up only snug. If pitching a cotton tent or pima tent,
this provides sufficient tolerance for humidity changes.

I prefer placing rear tent poles first, as the low end
offers less resistance to the wind. Pull poles rearward
about one inch beyond the perpendicular point. Then
the front poles are set, pulling them forward until
they are about one inch beyond the perpendicular point.
The resultant tautness makes for a well-pitched tent.
Sidewall guylines work best when pulled up and out
horizontally over a branch, packframe, or ice axe, and
then fastened to a tent pin. Occasionally a nearby tree
or branch will furnish the needed up-and-out pull that
makes a tent taut and roomy. A well-pitched tent is
achieved by adjusting guylines until the tent is as taut
and wrinkle free as possible. Convex or concave tent
sites complicate the process and prevent tautness. The
advantage of a well-pitched tent is that you don't have
to get up during the night in a soaking gale and do
what you should have done before you went to bed.

Tent pins are driven into the ground at an angle
slightly more than 90 degrees to the line attached to
them. Drive them in with hand, boot, or rock so that
they are below ground surface for maximum holding
power. It follows that since the pins are driven in at an
angle, they should be pulled out at the same angle, or
the pins will bend. Merely slide the tautline knot down
toward the pin to loosen the line and then pull on the
looped line attached to the pin. This system also prevents pins from becoming lost in the ground (e.g., as
each line is loosened, each pin is removed immediate-

ly). Pins frozen in the ground during the night come out better if first tapped in deeper and then immediately pulled out before they refreeze. Wire pins are not suitable for camping when frozen-ground conditions prevail, as they cannot be driven into the ground.

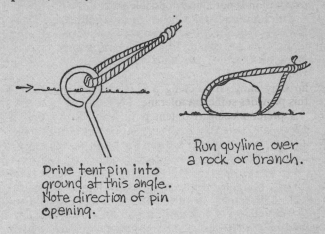

Drive tent pin into ground at this angle. Note direction of pin opening.

Run guyline over a rock or branch.

If pins cannot be driven into rocky soil, secure guy-lines to fairly large flat-bottomed basketball-size rocks by passing the line around the rock with the tension side (tent side) *down under the rock*. Spare ⅛-inch lines used to tie foam pads and ⅛-inch nylon shoe-laces may be pressed into service to anchor your tent for the night on a rocky site.

I've had only one experience with a collapsed tent, which occurred on the tail end of a tornado near Crystal Lake, Illinois. Five tents out of eight collapsed on a scout troop backpack when five aluminum tent poles collapsed in the middle of the night. Rather sad to hear the frightened, mournful cries emitting from the soggy piles of canvas. No one was injured, but neither could anyone say they weren't frightened. Had we known at the time we were victims of the rim winds of a tornado, we all would have been terrified. In this case ignorance was beneficial.

On our 1967 Teton trip, a storm blew down from

Mt. Moran, hissing and frothing as it steadily marched across Leigh Lake toward our trembling tent. My sons quickly reinforced every guyline with a heavy rock (we rocked our lines), while I lashed vertical branches around our tent pole to stiffen it for the impending blow. We dived into our tent on the windward side to hold it down just as the shock wave hit— that was something—we acually were lifted into the air for a microsecond. But lines and reinforced pole held; profuse prayers no doubt helped too.

Inspect Tent Sites

As you grow older you become more critical of your tent site and carefully inspect it for degree of slope, prevailing wind direction, morning sun angle in relation to eastern peaks, and twigs, pine cones and rocks that are guaranteed to end up under hip or shoulder. Small hollows may be filled before placing the tent on the ground, or, if you miss them, they may be filled after the tent is up by pushing handfuls of soil under the tent floor, or from inside your tent by placing dead (dirty) socks in the hollow. Bumps are evil sleep robbers, but sometimes you can curl around them. Sometimes.

Be extremely careful to pitch your tent away from any dead branch which might possibly fall on you during the night. You might even note the nearby tottering tree and avoid that location, as trees have to fall over eventually. Avoid potential rock or snow chutes. Stay out of dry river beds. You are perfectly free to assume that it will flood on the night you camp there. High ground is never too bad an idea, as water from rain or river generally will not run uphill.

A well-located tent precludes the necessity of digging trenches around a tent. Trenching is necessary in warfare, but today warfare will result if you create a blight on the landscape. Most Federal and state forests prohibit this practice, and if they don't, they should. At any rate, it is a waste of time and energy, and it indicates that you selected a poor campsite. Try again.

Packing a Wet Tent

If your tent was rained on during the night, but it is not raining when you get up, leave the tent up and shake and beat all the raindrops off as best you can. By the time breakfast is over, dishes are washed, and you are all packed up, your tent should be air dried even without sun. If your tent is essentially dry, place it inside your pack. If your tent is soaking wet, one suggestion is to lash your dripping home, horseshoe style, around the outside of your pack where it will not soak the essentials inside your pack.

Tent Colors

You might consider tent colors from the vantage point of how they look from inside with the sun shining on the sidewalls in the morning, the sought-for situation. Green is luminous and springtime; orange, coral, beige, and especially yellow are positively fall—joyous, like living inside a ray of sun. When viewed from the outside, tan or yellow tents look "homey" at night when a candle burns inside, sort of a magic glowing pumpkin. One authority says blue is best, as mosquitoes will be drawn to it rather than to your body. I would also assume blue is a happy summer-sky color when morning sunshine arrives.

Practice Pitching Your Tent

Try out your new mountain tent a few times in your backyard or nearby park to get used to setting it up and taking it down. Sprinkling with a garden hose will smooth out all the wrinkles as the tent dries. This might be an excellent opportunity to cut and fit your rectangular urethane foam pads to the inside tapered shape of your tent floor. Abutting pads should be placed over a center line marked on your tent floor to assist you in proper fitting of pads. When you are done, you'll have wall-to-wall comfort. After guylines have been lengthened or shortened, you'll be ready for a test run on your next car camp. Be sure to include your custom fit foam pad and mummy bag. You'll get a kick out of your simplicity of operation compared to your camping neighbor's safari giant. By slowly building up your expertise, you'll feel right at home when you embark on your first backpack.

Dry Tents Immediately

When you get back from your hike your tent should be immediately hung upside down in your heated basement or in your garage for a day or two until bone dry. Tent floor pin loops can be fitted over carefully placed nails driven into garage rafters or house floor joists and then you'll have an easy tent-drying spot for future trips. If no other drying place is available, drape your tent over a broom placed across two chairs in your living room. In dry climates pitch your tent in the hot sun of your backyard.

Be sure to gently shake out loose inside dirt so you have a clean tent for the next hike. Store your tent only after it is bone dry, then store it in a dry, heated location upstairs in the living area of your house. A neglected tent will mildew and rot quickly. It is not the material that causes a tent to rot; it is human forgetfulness.

Necessary Knots

Examples of Useful Knots

The small amount of nylon line carried is very useful; for example, the 15-foot length of ⅛-inch nylon line used to compress and secure your rolled foam pad may also be combined with your partner's 15-foot line and the combined 30-foot line thrown up and over a branch to suspend your nylon net food bag so that chipmunks and bears will not eat all your goodies.

Chipmunks are aggressive and are not afraid of people, while bears are timid and avoid people. I've been accosted by numerous chipmunks, but never by a bear. A black bear once demolished a campsite where we had drained off meat enzymes (juice) from freeze-dried pork chops. Connie and I made exceptional time getting away from that campsite. Judging from movies I have seen, bears can outrun and outclimb men. To paraphrase, "I hope that I shall never see a big black bear chasing me."

In suspending a nylon net food bag, the line is secured to the bag with a clove hitch; the two lines are joined together with a square knot (a fisherman's knot would even be more secure); and finally, the end of the line is tied to a branch with a clove hitch or perhaps a tautline. (A tautline is easier to tie as it is designed for a tight line.)

If you cannot secure your tent guyline with a tent pin, and if heavy rocks are not available, you may join your tent guyline to the 15-foot foam-pad line with a fisherman's knot, and tie to a group of shrubs.

Drying clothes is a common camp occurrence and

may best be handled with a bowline around one tree and a tautline around the other tree.

One knot you'll use each time you pitch your tent is a sliding tautline, and you will recall each tent line is secured to tent pull loops with a bowline.

In other words, the five necessary knots shown in this brief chapter are used repeatedly in backpacking. Knots are presented in order of manual dexterity required, from least to most. Practice at home and in car camps prior to your first backpack and you'll hike with increased confidence. If you think it's difficult to tie these knots, try sketching them.

SQUARE KNOT

Used to join together lines of
the same diameter and material,
such as shortened shoe lace,
bandana, sling or bandage.

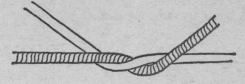

1. Twist

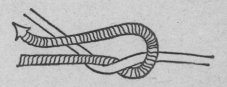

2. Loop (BLACK)

3. Over and out (WHITE)

To tighten: Pull black and white ends.

CLOVE HITCH

Used as a secure hitch around a branch or another line. For attaching tent guyline over pack frame, around branch or hanging food bag from a line.

1. Loop around, cross over.

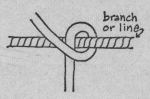

branch or line

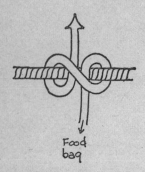

Food bag

2. Around again, <u>over</u> branch-then under crossing line.

To tighten: Squeeze loops together while pulling ends.

VARIATION:
Quick release clove hitch particularly handy for removing net bag from line.

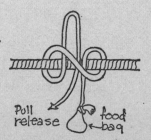

Pull release

food bag

FISHERMAN KNOT

Used to join two pieces of line together in a more positive manner than a square knot. For adding on to tent guylines.

1. Place ends of two lines parallel and make a loop around both.

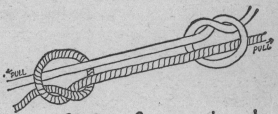

2. Same for opposite end.

To tighten: Tighten each loop separately then pull loops together. Tighten each loop again.

BOWLINE

Used to form a secure, nonslip loop in the end of a line. For attaching guylines to tent loops, one end of clothes line to a tree or one loop to another.

1. Loop over and thru.

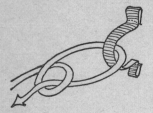

2. Up thru loop and over.

3. Around and over, down thru loop, and out.

To tighten: Snug up parts and pieces shown in dotted area.

TAUT LINE

Used as a secure sliding knot that tightens under load. For tightening tent guylines, loose end of a clothes line and pack lines.

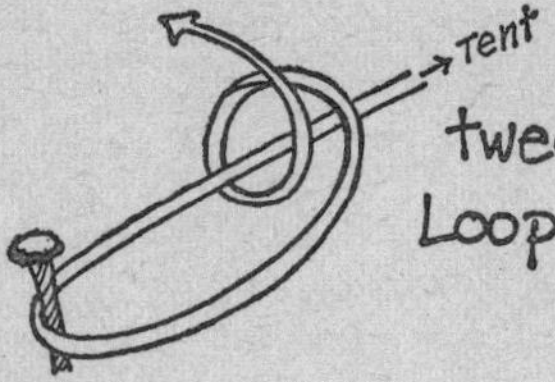

1. Pull line tight between tent & tent pin. Loop over.

2. Loop over again and cross over both Loops.

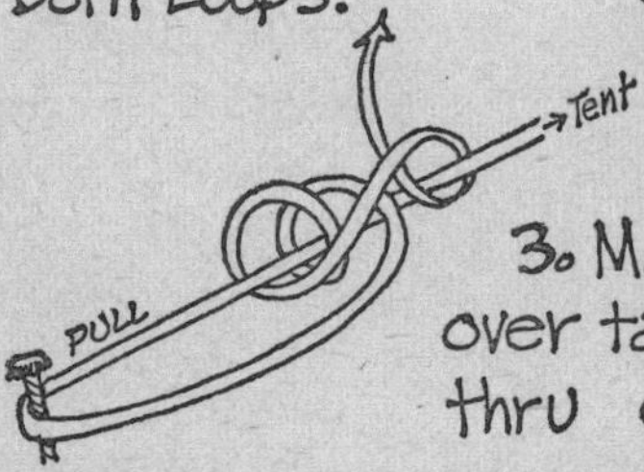

3. Make third loop over taut line and thru cross over.

To tighten: Snug up parts & pieces.
To tighten on tent - slide knot toward tent.

Variation: Same as above. Continue as shown by dotted line.

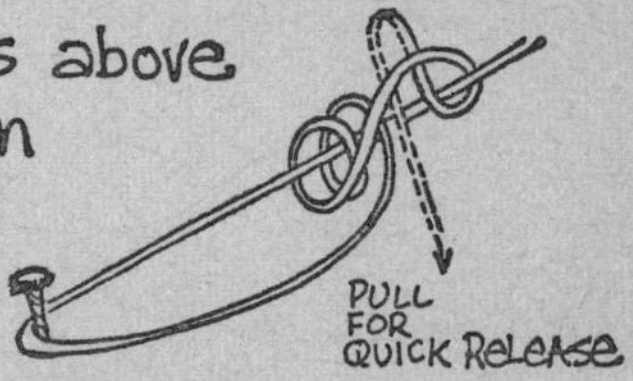

PULL FOR QUICK RELEASE

67

Packs, Rucksacks and Packframes

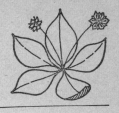

Excellent Choice of Packs

There are so many excellent packs on the market, available in various colors, materials, shapes, styles and price ranges, that shopping for a new pack is pure joy. Rather than attempt to endorse any one pack, let's see what packs do and how different packs can perform an excellent job for their owners. Individual needs and preferences are the most important factors in choosing your pack.

Rectangular Pack without Frame

I carry a patched 13-year-old, rectangular $8 Morsan cotton canvas bag similar to a scout "Yucca" pack with a suspension system similar to an old Army mountain pack; however, that's how the pack was when new, and it's been extensively modified in the intervening years. Pack size is 20 inches high, 16 inches wide, and 6 inches deep. Most of the load is carried on my shoulders. I apologize. Someday I'll relent and buy a scientifically designed pack, but not yet; there's a lot of good in that old pack.

The one-pound steel frame and canvas backband were removed years ago. The bellyband has been retained as it helps hold the pack against my body, providing more balance when scrambling across rockslides or crossing slippery logs. It's possible that some of the load might even be transferred to my hips.

Foam shoulder pads were added about two years ago. All heavy canvas webbing, steel buckles and steel "D" rings have been removed. A large flap from an old Yucca pack replaces the original skimpy cover. Nylon web loops were sewed to flap and pack body. Pack is closed with ⅛-inch nylon lines; a bowline is secured to the loop on the flap and passed through the loops on the pack body. A tautline quick-release knot secures the closure. Total weight for this stripped-down and modified pack is 2¾ pounds. One of these days I'll take this pack apart and use the pieces as a template and make a lightweight nylon pack that will weigh about 2¼ pounds.

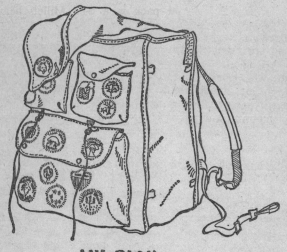

MY PACK

When Connie and I hike as a two-person team, my pack contains: sleeping bag, tent, tent poles, tent pins, spare-clothing bag, butane gas stove, spare fuel cartridge, and breakfast and supper bags. One large snap pocket on the rear contains my down jacket and rain jacket. Two smaller rear snap pockets are above the large pocket. One contains plastic water bottle, spoon and flashlight, while the other pocket contains plastic-wrapped first aid bag and 50 feet of ⅛-inch nylon line. Rolled and compressed foam pad is carried on top of my pack and under the flap. Frequently we carry a small American flag with tie tapes when we are in a mini-expedition mood.

For a week-long backpack my filled pack initially weighs about 33 to 35 pounds. Weight decreases with each meal consumed and we make a point of eating the heaviest-weight meals first.

Rucksack with Integral Frame

Connie's 3½-pound pack is a $17 Millet, heavy duty, gray canvas alpine rucksack, big on the plastic bottom with a small drawstring top covered by a small rounded flap with an inside zippered mapcase. Pack height is 16 inches and bottom dimensions are 17 inches wide by 7 inches deep. Beautiful gray leather straps and chrome buckles fasten flap to pack. A small molded plywood insert is in the back and a strip steel frame and canvas backband hold the pack slightly away from Connie's back, properly distributing some of the load to her hips. Straps for a bellyband were sewn on later, as they didn't come with the pack. The snug bellyband pulls the packload into the hips. A hauling loop is handy for hanging the pack in the closet. Padded shoulder straps were also included. All in all a most exquisite alpine pack; rugged, feminine, and professional, just like its owner.

The shape of Connie's pack dictates the order of packing; from large bottom to small top it contains: (bottom) sleeping bag, (middle) spare-clothing bag, (top) two nested cooking pots with plastic wrapped toilet paper placed inside and lunch-food bags on each side of the small pots. A centered pocket just accepts a compressed down jacket. Two other pockets are on each side of the center pocket. One holds a plastic water bottle and spoon, while the other holds hiking shorts and rain jacket. On a cloudy or foggy day the blue jeans are exchanged for hiking shorts in mid-trail at the first sign of the sun burning through. Rolled and compressed foam pad is carried on top of the pack under the pack flap. For a week's backpack Connie's filled pack initially weighs about 27 to 29 pounds.

CONNIE'S PACK

Packframe and Pack with Pockets

Chuck has a red 3⅞-pound REI welded aluminum senior packframe with a waterproof nylon pack; cost —$26. Pack is 21 inches high, 15 inches wide, 7 inches deep. Tom has a 3½-pound REI packframe and green nylon waterproof pack. Pack is 19 inches high, 14 inches wide, 7 inches deep. Both packs have zippered side pockets. Both use a waterproof nylon stuff sack to hold the sleeping bag below the pack. Load is properly distributed between shoulders and hips with backband and bellyband, although Chuck rarely uses the bellyband. Padded bellybands (or hipbands) may be added, which when worn snugly do an excellent job of transferring packweight to your hips, thus reducing weight on shoulders which is passed down your vertebrae. Padded bellybands might just be the answer for a hiker with a back problem.

72

Packframe and Pack with Zippered Compartments

Dick paid $30 for a used Gerry compartmentalized waterproof nylon pack which easily snapped off or on a bolted or screwed aluminum frame. Pack is 28 inches high, 15 inches wide, 10 inches deep at the bottom, 7 inches deep at the top. Pack and frame weigh three pounds. Frame has a nylon net backband and quick-release bellyband (if you fall into a stream it's awkward swimming with a loaded pack). Pack has excellent shoulder-hip weight distribution which could be improved further with a snug fitting padded bellyband. No pockets mar this fire engine-red pack. One zippered compartment popped under load and was graciously repaired at the manufacturer's expense.

All Packs Are Functional

As you may gather, each of us likes his own pack. Each pack, including frame, weighs about 3¼ pounds, plus or minus a half pound. All our packs are functional and all are trail-mileage tested.

Each pack fits the person who uses it, and that is the biggest test of a good pack. Another consideration: is it large enough to hold what you intend to carry? You may draw some conclusions from the pack sizes previously mentioned. Overall frame and pack weight are not so obvious, but you do have to carry your frame and pack. The handiness of a pack is related to the number and size of pockets or zippered compartments so that you can get at items easily as you need them along the trail. Finally, I believe each pack should express the owner's esthetic tastes as to shape, color, style and materials.

While our five packs differ in cost, style and materials, they transport the same clothing and equipment. In other words, our system of backpacking is not dependent upon a particular pack. Our system is the same even though the packs are different. Our packs are also representative of the three styles sold almost any place; rectangular, rucksack, and packframe, listed in order of carrying ease (worst to best) and increasing cost (least to most).

Frameless Pack and Packframes: Advantages vs Disadvantages

Without a frame my back sweats from contact with my pack. In hot sunny weather this is a pleasant sensation; in cool, cloudy weather this sensation is bone chilling, especially when trying to enjoy a brief rest. Not having detachable packframes, neither Connie nor I has to concern oneself with where to secure the frame at night; also, my pack rolls up easily and may be placed out of the way at the foot of our tent storage space, inside Connie's pack, or used under my foam pad as a pillow or hillside-slope adjuster.

With packframes Connie and our sons do not seem to have a back-sweating problem. Our sons' detached frames have been useful in serving as side supports for tent-sidewall guylines when fallen branches were not available. We secure the guylines up and over the horizontal bars of the frame to lift our tent sidewalls up and out, making our tiny tent tauter and roomier inside. Packframes distribute load better to your body, but packframes are bulkier and heavier than frameless packs.

Two-Person Pack Volumes

Connie and I, backpacking as a two-person team, are limited to about seven days away from a supply of food, as our combined pack volume will not hold more. Any two of our sons, with their larger volume packs and packing as a two-person team, could easily have pack volume for carrying food for two weeks, or, any one of our sons combined with either Connie or me would have pack volume for two weeks of food. This suggests that not only do you buy a pack to fit you as an individual, but that combined packs of a two-person team must have adequate volume, primarily to carry bulky food. As a practical matter, most backpacking vacations vary between one and two weeks. Far more two-three-four-day backpacking weekends are possible in proportion to one-two week backpacks. This suggests that large packs are impractical for most people *unless you are going on a two-week or longer trip*.

Perhaps, properly, I should carry more weight and Connie less, although there is historical evidence to suggest women should carry more. In certain American Indian cultures the women did most of the work (my wife says not much has changed), while the men canoed, hunted and fished. I don't know why the white man thought he could improve on that system.

Dick tells me that Eastern backpacking practice is to descend from the hills from time to time and replenish your food supply. In the state of Washington there are very few villages in the Cascade or Olympic Mountains. The Pacific Crest Trail crosses near Stehekin, where a small grocery store is located, but no grocery stores exist at Stevens Pass or Snoqualmie Pass. Perhaps the forest service or National Park Service should make arrangements for dehydrated and freeze-dried foods to be stocked at the ski resorts at both passes and at Stehekin for the convenience of Pacific Crest Trail backpackers.

Inside Bag vs Outside Bag

Connie and I must unpack our entire pack to reach the mummy bag inside on the bottom, a theoretical disadvantage only, since 99% of the time we unpack everything anyway when we make camp for the night. Once it was a disadvantage when Connie, Dick and I slept in a graveled parking lot overgrown with clover near the Chelan Boatworks in Chelan, Washington. We arrived about midnight so that Dick and I could catch the 8 A.M. boat that goes uplake about 50 miles through fjordlike rocky hills to Stehekin, Washington. We didn't need a tent as the night was warm, starry and clear, and the clover-scented parking lot far more inviting than a smoke-stenched motel room. Unpacking my entire pack to get at my sleeping bag was a disadvantage on this occasion, but there was compensation in the cool fragrance of clover as we talked and drifted off to sleep.

Waterproof Stuff Sacks

One advantage to a waterproof stuff sack, for carrying sleeping bags below a pack on a packframe, is that the stuff sacks may be used to transport water up to a dry campsite bypassed by other hikers. Chuck, Tom and I encountered this situation once on Orcas Island in the San Juan Islands. At that time we didn't carry a one-gallon collapsible water jug (two ounces) so we lined depressions in the ground with our waterproof

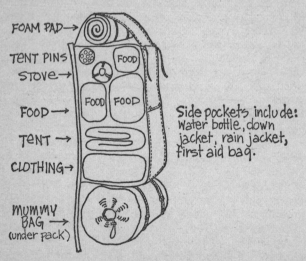

FOAM PAD →

TENT PINS
STOVE →
FOOD

FOOD FOOD

FOOD →

TENT →

CLOTHING →

MUMMY
BAG →
(under pack)

Side pockets include:
Water bottle, down
jacket, rain jacket,
first aid bag.

PACKING A PACK

rain jackets (coated side up) and filled these reservoirs with water toted uphill in our waterproof stuff sacks. By the next morning the local beetle swim team was in full practice in our pool.

Stuff sacks, rigged with a 15-foot nylon line used to compress your foam pad, also serve as a daypack if you, like me, are too weight conscious to pack a one-pound daypack inside your main pack. Dick rigged up such a temporary daypack when we explored some peaks in the Glacier Peak area of Washington. We carried first-aid bag, down jackets, water bottles and trail food in our makeshift pack, on our belts the ever-present cup, and in our pockets, match-safe, scout knife and map.

Packing a Pack

Regardless of what type of pack you own there is a certain generally agreed-upon manner in which to pack your belongings within a pack. The *Boy Scout Handbook* aptly refers to a pack as a "bag of bags." This is most descriptive since you carry within your pack (bag): food bags, clothing bags, first-aid bag, tent bag, tent-pole bag, tent-pin bag, and mummy bag.

Lightest, low-density items are packed on the bottom of the pack, medium-density items in the middle, and heavy- to high-density objects on top and close to the hiker's back. Generally this means your sleeping bag is inside your pack on the bottom or secured to the frame outside and underneath your pack. Next item to pack might be the light clothing bag, followed by the medium-weight rolled-up tent as you ascend higher within the pack. Heavy food bags would be placed on top of the tent inside the pack. Small and heaviest objects, such as tent pins and butane gas stove, are placed up highest toward the hiker's back, so that the weight doesn't pull out and back to unbalance the hiker.

Pockets located out and away from the hiker's body are best stuffed with low-density items such as down jacket, rain jacket, and first-aid bag. *High side pockets* are best for carrying heavy water bottles, *but in any case water bottles should be outside your pack* so they are easily accessible. Further, if the water bottle leaks it will leak outside your pack and not soak your dry clothing or food stored inside your pack.

COOKING POTS
W/ TOILET PAPER &
FOOD BAGS INSIDE
CLOTHING
DOWN JACKET
MUMMY BAG
WATER BOTTLE, ETC,
IN SIDE POCKET
FOOD

PACKING A PACK
LIKE CONNIE'S

Sit-down luncheon entree should be easily accessible, either on top center inside your pack or in a pocket outside your pack. Pack style determines which place is best. While the sit-down lunch entree is in the pack, your plastic bag of trail food is in your pocket, so that you do not need to stop for a bite, but may munch as you crunch along the trail.

Matches, Knife and Map Carried on Person

I favor carrying scout knife and matches safely in my pocket, since if for any reason my pack and I are separated, I know I have knife and matches to make a fire to keep myself warm, heat drinking water in my cup carried on my belt, and generally help me survive. If I were foolish enough to carry matches and knife in my pack, and if my pack dropped out of sight, I'd be in real trouble. Since *each partner* carries knife and matches on his person, we double the odds of survival without packs. For this same reason I rarely carry a map in my pack; I prefer my map in a buttoned shirt pocket. Survival expert Gene Fear told me that the ability to improvise is critical in a survival situation. (See Reference Books section at back of book.)

Packs, Food and Chipmunks

Food-filled packs may be suspended from a tree with ⅛-inch nylon line, or preferably empty packs may be stored inside your tent and food stored in a nylon net bag made from nylon mosquito netting. The net bag holding food is then suspended from a tree. This prevents chipmunks from eating holes in your pack, although they may sample your net bag. Removing food from your tent is critical, as chipmunks will ruin your sleep when they hurl themselves against your tent, attempting to eat your cereal, raisins, candy and other plastic-bagged goodies. Don't for five seconds believe that a tiny chipmunk can't smell food through a vinyl bag. Maybe you can't, but he can. Place your food up in the air each night if you plan to eat more than air in the morning.

If you camp overnight just west of Hart Lake, near Holden, Washington, there are some of the fattest, happiest, and most persistent chipmunks in the state. Dick and I suspended our food bag about 10 feet above ground, about 10 feet down from an overhead branch, and about five feet away from the tree trunk, branches, bushes or anything. That night at about 1 P.M. one pint-size trapeze flyer made it on top of our suspended net bag and ate his way through the nylon netting, several layers of vinyl bags, and managed to eat the ends off three fig bars before his joyous laughter and contented burping woke me up. Such a chipmunk deserved those cookies and would be a star performer on an Ed Sullivan TV circus spectacular. Dumb Animals?

How did the chipmunk do it? Can a chipmunk walk down a vertical line? At another location, Connie says she once saw a chipmunk leap about two feet to three feet horizontally onto our suspended food bag. They sure like Ju-Jus and cashew nuts. It's fun to watch them eat, right up to the moment when it dawns on you that they are eating your lunch.

Personalize Your Pack

Packs may be personalized with embroidered emblems obtained in certain national parks and certain ski shops in or near wilderness areas or ski resorts. It would be nice if all national parks and Regional Forest Service headquarters would sell patches commemorating wilderness trails in their jurisdiction. Over the years it is fun to collect these colorful emblems and sew them on your pack in memory of fun hikes in that area.

Boy scouts may earn these emblems for participating in certain hikes and special camps. My sons and I treasure a "Blackhawk Trail" emblem awarded for a beautiful 20-mile hike near Oregon, Illinois, plus the required reading of *The Shining Trail,* by Iola Fuller, a most fascinating book on Saulk and Fox Indian life and lore. If you read carefully enough you might even learn how to make stone arrowheads. "Shining Trail" refers to the sun shining on the river which was the Indians' canoe route, or water trail; hence, shining trail.

Don't Need vs Need to Have

After returning from a backpack spread out all your belongings on the floor and note the items you never used. Other than the first-aid bag, do not again bring the items you didn't use; you have proved you don't need them. Also, you might note what you didn't bring, did get along without, but will never forget to bring again. For example, your spoon.

Some items are not really essential, but if they only weigh a few ounces and materially increase your enjoyment, why not include them? Life is too short to abandon all personal pleasure, for example, a paperback, *Jonathan Livingston Seagull,* would be great to share on a rainy day in a tiny tent.

Eventually packing up for a backpack trip will become automatic, with food purchase, premixing and bagging being the principle concerns.

Care of Packs

Sweaty packs, or dunked packs, should be aired and sun dried at each break and particularly after you arrive in camp. Once you are home, packs should be shaken clean, dried and brushed, and loose threads or opened seams repaired before your next backpack. Inspect fastenings, zippers, and shoulder-strap attachment to pack. Oil and resin stains should be cautiously removed with turpentine; remember, lacquer thinner will dissolve nylon pack fabric.

Since packs contain all your belongings, it follows that care should be exercised in handling packs. Sitting on loaded packs could burst a stitched seam, or worse, could burst a bag of powdered milk inside your pack. Packs should be lowered gently to the ground, not dropped, as you might break a welded joint, bend the frame out of proper alignment, break off the control knob on your butane stove or rupture your filled plastic water bottle.

When handing a loaded pack to another person, avoid swinging the pack by its shoulder straps; hold the pack underneath. Some hikers momentarily relieve the load on their shoulders by sort of jumping the pack up in the air for a second. The pack isn't hurt going up, but the sudden stop coming down just might tear off your shoulder strap. Avoid sudden loading of the pack shoulder straps.

Carefully close zippers and equally carefully open snap fasteners; no need to tear them off the pack. Most equipment is adequately made and will function well if given half a chance.

Be especially careful to avoid bending the telescoping, sectional aluminum tent poles, as they never

81

telescope quite so freely after having been bent. Once a scout helped me unload my pack out of a truck, dropped my pack upside down on the ground, and drove the protruding tent poles right through the bottom of my pack. A yellow canvas patch is sewn over the wound with commemorative somber black thread.

What's Cooking?

Excellent Meals from Frugal Gear

Some of the most enjoyable moments of a backpacking involve food: snacking along the trail, nibbling mini-lunches alongside a talkative waterfall, leisurely eating breakfasts in bed inside your sunny tent, and preparing gourmet feasts by a campfire at the end of a demanding day. In spite of the frugal cooking gear, excellent meals can be prepared quite simply.

For a two-person hiking team the only cooking equipment needed is two cups, two spoons, two pots, nylon net bag, butane gas stove, spare fuel cartridge, nylon pot scrubber, scout knife, match-safe filled with self-striking large wooden matches (paper matches absorb water and may not light), and an optional but recommended one-gallon collapsible water jug with a screw-on top. Collapsible jugs are inflated by blowing into them.

You can get along just fine with one pot; however, it limits meals to some form or other of stew. I enjoy stew, but not *every* night. If you do decide to take just one pot, make it large enough (3½ quarts) to slip over the end of your rolled, compressed sleeping bag and you'll never even miss the space. Personally, I like to take two cooking pots, as it does permit more creative cookery.

Stainless Steel Cup

Best overall cup to take is the Sierra stainless steel cup, which is cool to the lips when the cup is filled

SIERRA CUP

with hot liquids. Cup doubles as a soup bowl and dinner plate. Its broad flat bottom permits use as a mini fry pan or cooking pot, and it is very stable when placed on the ground. The curved wire handle may be hooked through your belt so that the cup is always handy for getting a drink when an inviting stream tumbles across your trail. Hook the cup over your belt so that the inside of the cup faces your body, not the other way around, or you'll lose your cup. Your stainless steel cup will not burn, warp, crack or bend. It is not prone to dent and may be easily cleaned, as it is without seams or rivets.

Taking a drink of water from a tiny stream along the trail is to me one of the better experiences of life. Did you ever stop to think of the few areas in America where you may take a drink of cold, crystal-clear water directly from a stream and not give one second's thought to the water's purity? Obviously each hiker will do all in his power to keep those streams clean so that they will always be available to offer drinking water to other passersby.

Knife and Spoon

Stainless steel spoons will perform every function of a table knife or table fork, neither of which you need. Spoons spread, cut, stir, ladle, and lift. Carry a scout pocket knife which will cut, slice, peel, skin, spread, open cans, clean fingernails, trim toenails, perforate leather belts, and when well sharpened on a hard smooth stone picked up along the trail will shave you clean, although admittedly leaving you nicked, raw and shaking.

Cooking Pots

Cooking pots are manufactured in "soft" (dull) and "hard" (shiny) aluminum. The "hard" will wear and clean better than the "soft" aluminum. Pots should have bail handles similar to those on pails. Excellent meals may be cooked in one pot; however, two nesting pots, 1½ quarts and one quart, provide more options.

Years ago we only used one pot, which is adequate, though it does limit your culinary creativity. Our family enjoys cooking and eating so we carry a full line of gourmet cooking equipment; namely, two pots. One reason we carry two pots is that breakfast fruit may be cooked the previous evening in the small pot and covered by press-fitting the upside down large pot totally over the small pot. This rainproof assembly is slipped into your nylon mosquito-net bag and suspended from a tree so that insects cannot eat your next morning's feast. Be sure you rig this swinging delicacy so that the pot will not tip in the wind and spill your cooked fruit.

Nylon Net Bag

We have obliquely mentioned our nylon net bag (one-half ounce). Its flat finished size is about 18 inches wide by about 20 inches high and is secured by a small diameter nylon drawstring tied in a loop so that the line will not slip out of its casing. Strength, light weight, small volume, and bug resistance are the bag's main features. Material may be purchased by the yard from camping suppliers. I believe Connie made two bags from one lineal yard of 40-inch-wide material. Be sure you get strong nylon mosquito netting.

The uses of nylon net bags are many. Originally the bags were made so washed and rinsed dishes could air dry in an insect-free suspended bag. Additional uses include wearing the bag as a protective head covering

HOW TO MAKE A NYLON NET BAG

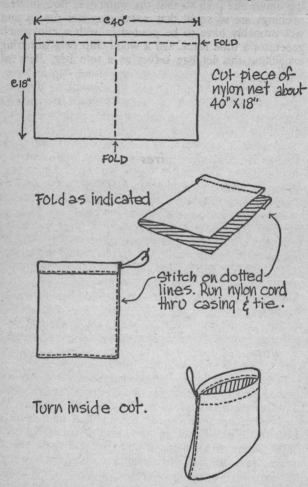

Cut piece of nylon net about 40" X 18"

FOLD as indicated

Stitch on dotted lines. Run nylon cord thru casing & tie.

Turn inside out.

to frustrate mosquitoes. Washed dishes may be placed inside and dunked in boiling water on car camps when many dishes are used. We used a nylon net bag as a strainer to remove algae from lake water near Ely, Minnesota, when on a canoe trip. Place bag over water-bottle opening and then poke bag material into opening about one inch so that the water will flow in. Net openings are so small that water may not run in and will probably have to be poured in with a cup which generates a little force. On a wood-chip twig-gathering expedition the net bag serves as a tote bag. Bags of food may be placed inside the nylon net bag and suspended high above ground in an attempt to discourage chipmunks and other hungry critters from eating your food.

Types of Cooking Fires

We use both wood cooking fires and a butane gas stove for cooking meals.

Breakfasts are usually eaten cold inside our tent; as we wait ℉or the sun we warm our home. Water is heated (not boiled) over our butane stove for hot coffee, hot Start, or hot Russian tea. Egg bacon-bar breakfasts are best over a wood fire and usually reserved for our "easy" day or our "day off."

Trail lunches are always eaten cold; hence, we do not use a fire of any kind. We could if need arose, but looking back I can recall only one lunch where I prepared hot soup over a butane stove, and that was for two guests of Tom's from Los Angeles who have never seen splashing waterfalls fed from snowfields. I acted like a Chamber of Commerce guide-cook for our delighted guests, Mike Ehrman and Alan Crandall, on a short two-mile hike from Sunrise, near Mt. Rainier.

Suppers are a toss up. If we are tired and daylight is short, we use our butane gas stove. If we arrive early in the afternoon we prefer a wood fire. On "easy" days, or on "days off" we generally use a wood fire for supper.

Butane Gaz Stove

We enjoy cooking over a small wood fire, but if we cook in our tent, or are lazy, or forest-fire danger is high, we cook over our butane Gaz stove that has a fuel cartridge good for about three hours of continuous cooking. The stove weighs only 1½ pounds, including filled fuel cartridge. Start your hike with a fresh fuel cartridge, and carry a 10-ounce spare fuel cartridge good for another three hours of cooking. The butane Gaz stove is inexpensive, rugged, dependable, has easy-to-replace fuel cartridges, and has worked well for our family in the Midwest and Pacific Northwest from sea level to 11,500 feet. We own two stoves and randomly use one or the other; we have had no malfunction in five to six years of use. Our first stove has been used in Illinois, Wisconsin, Michigan, Canada, Minnesota, Wyoming, Idaho, Oregon and Washington.

If the burner head were manufactured in a rough sand texture you could strike a match on the burner head and avoid the search for stones or the self-immolation act of striking a match on your fly zipper.

A butane Gaz stove will not leak gasoline into your pack, as most gasoline stoves and almost all gasoline storage bottles will do, and it is, I believe, considerably safer than a gasoline stove. Our family long ago abandoned two different makes of gasoline stoves that were unreliable and potentially dangerous. A butane stove will not flare up as a gasoline stove will, which means a butane stove is safer for use inside a tent. Butane stoves function similarly to gas ranges used at home; light it and turn the knob for more or less heat.

Butane stoves will not operate below freezing temperatures, as the butane will not vaporize. Thus, the usefulness of a butane stove used inside a tent is limited to outside temperatures of about 25-30 degrees, well within the summer conditions applicable throughout this book.

Butane stoves must be protected from the wind, which robs heat or blows out the flame. Placing the stove inside your tent, in the vestibule, works fine in high wind. Close down the flaps a bit and check that horizontal heat or flame will not damage your tent sidewalls. If stove is used outside, depressions in the ground, hollow tree stumps, piled rocks, or a rain jacket draped over packframe will also shield the flame from wind. We no longer pack the bulky "X" support for the Gaz stove, instead we burrow the stove into the soil, sand, or pile rocks around it to stabilize the stove when used *outside* the tent. Cooking inside the tent requires more awareness of potential tipping. When inside a tent I suggest that one hiker hold the cooking pot bail handle while the other stirs. Move cautiously. If you are cooking inside the tent always open the tent flaps slightly to vent fumes. Be intelligent and note the relationship of nylon netting, sidewalls, clothing, and your own hair to the flame when you use the stove inside your tent. Avoid sudden movements.

Three-Rock Wood-Burning Cooking Fire

Two essentially flat-topped rocks are placed on the ground about two to four inches apart to support the two cooking pots. Rocks are placed so that the space between them is tapered and lines up with the prevailing winds. The widest opening faces the wind. The narrow opening is adjusted to fit the one-quart pot and the larger opening is fitted to hold the 1½-quart pot. Rocks are leveled by sight, or if you prefer precision, with water-filled pot.

WIND

Use a stick to dig a trench between the rocks, about four inches deep and ten inches long. A third vertical rock is placed at the narrow end of the two rocks and serves as a chimney between itself and the side of the small pot. In the morning, when the wind reverses itself, merely switch the chimney rock to the other end.

Small cooking fires require almost constant feeding with finger-thick sticks. Hottest fire is on the chimney side, good for boiling, and coolest fire is at the other end, facing the wind, good for simmering.

If rocks are not available, dig a four-inch deep by four-inch wide by ten-inch long trench.

I'm not sure if any Indian actually said this, but the story goes that an Indian commenting on the early Western pioneer said, "White man build big fire and stand way back; Indian build little fire and stand up close." Makes sense to me. Connie and I frequently cook an entire meal from wood chips gathered from some overzealous axe-wielding camper. We usually do this in conjunction with tidying up our home away from home.

When leaving your campsite, fill in the four-inch by ten-inch hole and cover the filled hole with the three cooking rocks. Leave surplus fuel piled vertically against the cooking rocks, handy for the next camper. (Vertical sticks shed rain better than horizontal sticks.)

Cleaning Pots

Nylon pot scrubbers are excellent. You do not need soap unless you are a compulsive clean type. Soap-pad scrubbers are horrible, as soapy goo gets over everything, including you. Enjoy your wilderness; don't lather it. Try fine sand and soil to rub your cups and pots clean. Similar to Lava soap. Rinse the dirt away. If burned food or resin is on the bottom of the cooking pot, rub on sandy soil. For heaven's sake don't clean blackened pot bottoms, just slip them inside your nylon net bag when packing.

Menus and Shopping Lists

First step in food preparation is writing down preferences for meals on a per-day basis for each day you will be hiking, plus allow food for one extra day (three meals) in case bad weather delays you. Translate menus into shopping lists. You will note from the food lists at the end of this chapter that we buy only individual dehydrated and freeze-dried foods so that we may put together meals exactly as we like them. Why pay for items you don't like just because they are packaged and sold as a "four-man meal"? Arrange purchased food into piles on the floor, sofa or table, representing each meal so that you may visually note what you forgot to buy.

You may wish to redistribute your food at this time from a big meal to a skimpy meal. Eventually all individual and bulk items are on hand and both hiking partners agree that potential meals look great.

Premixing and Packaging Individual Foods

Next comes premixing and packaging of food in plastic bags; for example, instant pudding mix is emptied from its cardboard box and paper liner and placed inside a small plastic sandwich bag. Ordinary plastic sandwich bags without special fold lock work best. Add proper amount of powdered milk to the plastic bag of pudding mix. Tear off a small piece of pudding label, listing flavor, and on the reverse side write down the correct amount of water to add to the pudding mix. Another example: Start powdered orange-drink mix is emptied from its can equally into two small sandwich bags handy for two breakfasts for two people. Premix and package other foods in a similar manner. Remove cardboard boxes and only pack the aluminum foil envelopes of dehydrated soup. No need to repackage soup envelopes.

We buy bulk freeze-dried coffee, powdered cream

(actually powdered chemicals—I do not know why I use them), and instant tea with sugar and lemon. These items are measured out on an estimated use-per-meal basis and placed in medium-size individual plastic bags loosely tied in a loop. These plastic bagged bulk items, plus sugar, are placed within one large doubled plastic "staple" bag.

Packaging Individual Meals

After menus have been decided upon, and individual foods premixed and bagged, each meal may be assembled into one large plastic bag marked "SUPPER," "BREAKFAST," or "LUNCH," a very precise system highly recommended for novice backpackers as it eliminates numerous parts and pieces and thereby reduces confusion. You have choice as to which supper, but not the components within the supper, which were predetermined at home to each party's satisfaction. I usually carry all breakfast and supper bags, while Connie carries all lunch bags, as this arrangement seems to best fit our pack space.

Entree System of Packaging Meals

Another food-packing system advocated and used by Dick when he was a canoe counselor at Camp Nebagamon for boys near Duluth, Minnesota, is to place all parts and pieces of all suppers in one or two large plastic bags. For example, place all dehydrated vegetables and all desserts in one large plastic bag and place all freeze-dried meat and canned fish in another large plastic bag. To assemble a particular supper, simply select your meat or fish entree and then select your vegetables and dessert. Condiments are taken from the "staple" bag. This system permits freedom in on-the-spot selection of individual components of the meal.

The entree system is accurate as long as you select one meat or one fish, two vegetables, and one dessert, or whatever number of items *you* preplanned per meal.

One advantage to the entree system is that you may rearrange your daily food allowance; for example, decide to forego Start for breakfast, but save it and combine it with lemon tea to make Russian tea for supper, or, omit cooked fruit for supper dessert and have it the following morning for breakfast. This simpler entree system is well suited to saving a bit of food here and there to build up extra meals in case bad weather keeps you out on the trail a day or two more than you planned. It's rather comforting to know you are ahead on food rather than behind. Connie and I, and Dick and I, have tried the entree system here in Washington and like its simplicity both in camp and when packing meals. Try both individual-meal system and entree system to see which you like best.

Lunch

The easiest meal to prepare and eat is lunch, which can be eaten in two different manners.

First method is to carry your entire lunch in your pocket and eat it as you walk the trails. This saves considerable time over the second method, a sit-down lunch, and provides your body with small amounts of energy continuously over a long period of time. In this manner, your leg muscles and digestive system are not in competition with one another, but rather digestion (and energy) are supportive of legs.

Trail Food

Food eaten on the trail is known as trail food and is carried in individual plastic bags. A simple trail-food lunch might be a chunk of hard salami, chunk of cheese, and a handful of raisins-peanuts-candy mixture of your liking. Trail lunches might begin at 9 or 10 A.M. and continue throughout the day until 3 or 4 P.M. Trail food is especially pleasant on demanding upgrades as this instant energy helps pull you through. One of my former explorer scouts, Pete Stellmach, now at the University of Colorado, tied a piece of salami around his neck on an explorer post rock climb and nibbled when he had a free moment or two.

ENTREE SYSTEM
OF PACKING FOOD

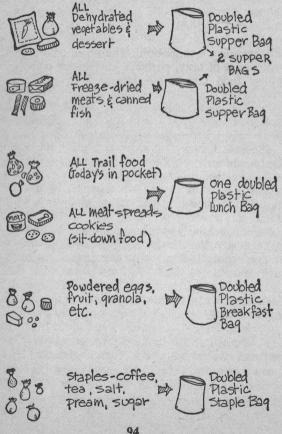

ALL Dehydrated vegetables & dessert → Doubled Plastic Supper Bag ↳ 2 SUPPER BAGS

ALL Freeze-dried meats & canned fish → Doubled Plastic Supper Bag

ALL Trail food (Today's in pocket)

ALL meat-spreads cookies (sit-down food) → one doubled plastic Lunch Bag

Powdered eggs, fruit, granola, etc. → Doubled Plastic Breakfast Bag

Staples-coffee, tea, salt, Pream, sugar → Doubled Plastic Staple Bag

The essential idea of trail food is its nonspoiling character and ease of eating. Substitute whatever you like for cheese and salami, as long as it is nonspoiling and can be eaten with fingers while you hike (e.g., pepperoni sticks, beef sticks, beef jerky). Mixes of raisins-peanuts-candy could be as varied as your imagination and taste. I like jellied candies, such as Ju-Jus; on the other hand, coated M & M's are good too. Both candies are nonmelting and can be eaten with the fingers. If you don't like raisins, try other dried fruits. Raisins happen to be loaded with energy and are also low cost. Dry-roasted cashews are terrific and easy to eat, but are not low cost. As you can well see, this could turn into a delightful subject—sort of a personal traveling smorgasbord. The name of the game is small pieces of tasty, portable, easy-to-eat energy.

Trail food (raisins-nuts-candy) is prepackaged at home in small plastic bags. I prefer to loosely tie the trail-food bags so that they may be easily opened on the trail. One bag per person per lunch. You can have a lot of fun by hoarding your last piece of candy and dramatically eating it at 4 P.M. after a tough uphill hike, hours after your partner has eaten his last bite, or, he can practice one-upsmanship by nibbling his last piece right in front of you as you are snuggled in your sleeping bag ready for sleep, hungrily eyeing his triumph.

For all premixed or prepacked food bags I slowly and carefully suck the air out of the bag to reduce its volume, twist the plastic into a cord and tie an overhand knot in the cord. Try not to inhale powdered food, as it may be harmful to your health. Cut off surplus plastic cord from all bags to reduce the volume of bagged food. If you tie the bags as suggested, you will not need metal ties, which could end up as litter on the trail. Save empty plastic food bags and burn them at your first available campfire, or pack them out. By now none of us are so thoughtless as to throw plastic bags along the trail, or anywhere else for that matter. Most Washington trails are clean, particularly as you get farther and farther from the trailhead. The trail behind you is a testimony to the professional backpacker you are becoming.

Trail Food and Sit-Down Lunch

The second lunch style favored by our family involves a split system. Part of lunch is trail food eaten on the trail during the day, and part is a sit-down lunch, such as one tiny can of ham spread or similar spreads shared with your partner and spread over either bread, crackers, seasoned Ry-Krisp, or chocolate chip or fruit-filled cookies. It's fun to pack a tiny loaf of bread and enjoy real bread for breakfast and lunch and supper for one or two days until it's all gone. The incongruity of fresh bread in the wilderness doubles its appeal. Most fruit-filled cookies make excellent bread substitutes and are loaded with all the good things you like. They keep well and do not crumble. Purists will rise in protest; they can eat their compressed tasteless crackers; I'll eat rye bread and fruit cookies as long as they last.

Luncheon brews are generally water, although you may wish to carry a few plastic bagged half-cans of Start for special lunches after rough uphill switchbacks. Liptons 1.8-ounce packet of dehydrated tea with sugar and lemon and vitamin C offers the most for the least weight, although Start orange drink is a close runner up for flavor. Experiment and take what you like. One 1.8-ounce packet of Lipton tea will make four cups, regardless of what the directions state. Flatten packet and fold in half so that half of the tea is on one side of the fold, the other half on the other side. Tear open one corner of the packet and pour instant tea into your pint plastic water bottle. Shake and serve. Save remaining half of tea for another time.

Even though Start and Lipton tea are relatively lightweight, several bags or foil packets begin to add up, so water is generally the luncheon beverage. You're not being deprived; perhaps the only pure water in America is the mountain water you are drinking while backpacking.

For the economy minded it is good to know that all lunch materials are available on your grocers' shelves.

Breakfast

Breakfasts are partially obtained from your grocer and partially from dehydrated or freeze-dried foods obtained in camping stores. Breakfast can generally be classified into cooked and noncooked. Good meal planning might include 50% cooked and 50% noncooked breakfasts. One advantage of noncooked is that the entire breakfast may be prepared inside the tent during a hard-driving rain, without the need for a fire. Another advantage of noncooked breakfasts is that they are usually quick, and there are many times when you'll wish to get up, eat, and move right out. Noncooked breakfasts also conserve butane fuel for the Gaz stove. Cooked breakfasts cost you trail time, although this depends on your objectives for a particular day.

Noncooked Breakfast

Examples of a noncooked breakfast: two portions of Start orange drink packed in a plastic bag, two portions of breakfast cereal in a plastic bag, two portions of cookies (or bread if you are lucky) in a plastic bag, individual jam packets and freeze-dried coffee with sugar and/or powdered cream or hot Russian tea or hot tea with sugar and lemon. Russian tea is made by combining orange Start with lemon-sugar tea. Delicious. You could eliminate the hot drink in favor of a cold drink to save time, but if you are in the mountains I'll bet you won't.

Each plastic bag containing two portions is divided equally into the two cups. If you've never eaten breakfast out of just one cup, a few suggestions may be helpful. When eating cold cereal, first mix the powdered milk in your cup, adding water to taste, *then add the cereal to the milk*. The other way around is chaotic.

We have tried premixing dry cereal and powdered milk at home and it has generally been pretty sad. The cereal and milk separate, and you end up with watery cereal or dusty milk.

Obviously, you have discovered that you are eating in courses: the first course was orange Start drink, second course was cereal with milk, and the third course was hot coffee. A noncooked breakfast satisfies the urge of lazy hikers who prefer to eat without getting out of their cozy sleeping bags.

Noncooked breakfast cereal should be rather dense and nutritious, such as Grape Nuts, Granola, or Franola (rolled oats, soya oil, brown sugar, honey, wheat germ, date flakes, apricot flakes, prune flakes, cashews, almonds, salt and pure vanilla flavoring). Most dry cereals crush into dust and are not worth packing. A third to a half cup of dry cereal is about right for one person. Determine at home how much you really eat. No point in carrying a half cup if you can eat only a third cup. Plan on one liquid cup of powdered milk per person to use on cereal; this means one-third cup of powdered milk per person. Allow one or two pieces of bread or cookies per person. Since one can of Start yields four cups, one can may be divided into two plastic bags; one bag for two people for one breakfast, and the other bag for two people for another breakfast. Plastic bagged two-person portions are divided into cups at breakfast.

With a noncooked breakfast the only "cooking" is mixing water with powdered milk in your cup and then adding dry cereal, mixing water with Start in your cup, and mixing water with coffee, tea, or Russian tea. Water may be heated, not boiled (avoid scalding yourself), for hot breakfast drinks or hot milk over cereal. If most of your camping has been at lower elevations, you may not appreciate the satisfaction of hot milk on cereal on a cold or chilly morning at higher elevations. To make sure we're on the same wave length, heat only water in the cooking pot. *Do not mix coffee, tea, milk or chocolate with water in the cooking pot.* All mixing takes place in your cup.

If you've planned ahead you can take your swinging applesauce out of your tree and warm it for breakfast.

Cooked Breakfast

Cooked breakfasts offer a good deal of delicious variety.

Instant precooked cereals such as rice, oatmeal, Cream of Wheat, Ralston, etc. may be simply and quickly prepared. At home carefully determine the dry-measure quantity of cooked cereal that you can eat. Rice, for example, expands phenomenally when cooked.

Dehydrated fruit abounds: peaches, pears, apples, raisins, and apricots; however, certain freeze-dried peaches and especially strawberries unfortunately taste like plastic and are to be avoided. Cooked fruit mixed with or served over cereal is good. Cooked fruits tend to boil down and will burn unless water is added frequently. Add a little sugar to your fruit and boil down so that juice is thick, but do not burn. *For best results stir frequently and add water frequently.*

Foil-wrapped, precooked bacon bar is delicious mixed with canned dehydrated eggs. Eggs are best scrambled and do not need salt, as the bacon will contribute sufficient salt. Canned freeze-dried instant ham cubes or pork patties are also excellent with dehydrated potatoes or eggs, or both.

Bacon bar is purchased precooked. Generally it is crushed into crumbs and added to cereal, eggs, potatoes, soup, salads, or whatever. It could be eaten as is. One three-ounce bacon bar split between two people is a lot of bacon, since it was originally 16 ounces of fresh bacon which was cooked, then drained of fat. Basically, only the meat is left, which makes it very tasty and very filling.

Canned dehydrated eggs taste best mixed with (1) bacon bar, (2) ham cubes, or (3) pork patties, in that order, as the meat camouflages the dehydrated-egg taste. For best results mix egg powder with a small amount of water and keep mashing the lumps, adding a little more water, mashing the lumps, etc. until the correct amount of water has been added and lumps are long gone. After 10-15 minutes of loving care, you'll have a smooth lump-free egg slurry *which is 98% of the secret of preparing good (well, almost good) dehydrated eggs.* Scrambled eggs are formed when the mixture solidifies on the bottom of the pot, so continuously scrape bottom, sides and corners of the pot with your spoon as you cook. Do a thorough job or the eggs will stick to the pot and burn.

When eggs are almost done, add bacon, ham, or pork, previously prepared. Do not add salt, as it is absorbed from the meat. If the eggs in the bottom of the pot are inadvertently scorched (meaning you goofed), do not scrape, but rather stir above the burned portion so the burned flavor does not permeate the entire pot of eggs. *The key is to mix well, scrape pot bottom constantly, and camouflage the dehydrated-egg flavor with bacon, ham, or pork.*

Toast makes the breakfast and coals from a burned down wood fire make toast. Impale bread on a clean whittled stick in one corner and hold bread close to coals. Change corners and reverse sides frequently. Another even simpler method is to blow ashes off coals and lay bread directly on the clean coals. Turn bread every few seconds and rotate as required. Slightly burned toast may be scraped, just like at home. Badly burned toast is a sad occasion, since bread is a luxury available only for the first two or three days of your hike.

Coffee, hot chocolate, tea, Russian tea and Start are some of the breakfast drinks available. (Again, heat *only* water in the cooking pot, *never* coffee or hot chocolate; *all mixing is done in your cup.*)

Cook and Eat in Courses

It may occur to you that a lot of cooking is being done on one tiny stove and two small pots. True. The trick is to cook and eat in courses. For example:

1. Heat water in pot (do not boil).
2. Prepare cold or hot Start in cups.
3. Soak instant pork patties or ham cubes in their opened cans with hot water, bend down partially opened lid so that meat is submerged in hot water.
4. One person mixes and cooks eggs in pot. Drain water from pork or ham and add water to egg slurry if you are short on water. Add meat to partially cooked eggs, or crumble bacon bar into eggs. Serve eggs and meat in cups.
5. If you have a wood fire, one person makes toast to eat with eggs and spreads jam on toast. Keep toast warm on a rock by the fire. If you don't have a fire, enjoy bread and jam.
6. Clean egg pot and heat water for coffee.
7. Clean any leftover (joke) egg and meat out of cups and serve hot coffee.
8. Warm up fruit cooked night before and serve in cups.
9. Clean cups and pots and rinse in cold water (good), warm water (better), or boiling water (best).

You get the idea; cook and serve in courses, just like a fine restaurant.

Gourmet One-Pot Suppers

Suppers are especially welcome after backpacking all day, and seem to work out best when cooked over an open wood fire, and eaten slowly in courses while watching flickering coals blend into the sunset.

You may wish to start supper with a soothing drink. Choose from hot or cold Start, hot or cold lemon-sugar tea, or hot or cold Russian tea. If the evening is warm and snow is at hand, you'll naturally ice your drink.

Perhaps Maggi dehydrated mushroom soup or Lipton dehydrated potato soup with seasoned Ry-Krisp would be welcome as your next course. Both of these exceptional soups are made by merely boiling water. Mushroom soup should be boiled until mushrooms are tender, regardless of what the directions state. The potato-soup recipe suggests using milk; however, it is equally good made with water only. If you *do not need* soup stock for stew or gravy, make soup thicker; if you *do need* soup stock, make soup thinner by adding more water. Serve soup in cups.

Salads Are Simple to Prepare

Buy dehydrated vegetable-stew mix and soak one-half of mix in each stainless steel cup about one hour before supper. Place a small flat rock over each cup to force buoyant salad mix down into the water and to discourage inquisitive birds or curious chipmunks.

The best salad-dressing mix I have been able to locate is a low-cal packet of mix that only requires the addition of vinegar and water. One small packet will make four servings of dressing, enough for two meals. Since water is plentiful in the mountains, the only special item to transport is a few tablespoons of vinegar accurately measured at home to provide four servings. We carry vinegar in a four-ounce plastic baby bottle. Simply invert the rubber nipple to form a gasket that tightly seals so that it won't spill in your pack.

To prepare salad dressing, pour off one-half of vinegar into a plastic bag (or on top of a bag if you do not have any empty bags) and temporarily set it aside. Add the required amount of water to vinegar in baby bottle. Empty one-half of the packet of salad-dressing mix into the baby bottle containing the vinegar and water. Cap the bottle and shake vinegar-water mix vigorously.

Drain water from soaked vegetable-stew mix and pour one-half of salad dressing over each cup of salad. Resultant salad is a bit crunchy but quite tasty.

Carefully clean salad-dressing mix from baby bottle and when clean pour vinegar stored in the plastic bag back into the baby bottle so you are ready for another salad on another day. Likewise, remember to save the remaining one-half of the salad-dressing mix in its packet.

One deluxe salad variation involves adding a can of tuna or two small cans of reconstituted freeze-dried instant ham cubes for an excellent tuna or ham salad. Makes an entire meal and is delicious on a warm night.

On your first night out you might go one step farther and add one fresh tomato, which you have carried with tender loving care. Heavy weight can of tuna and tomato are eaten the first night out, which reduces the food load you will carry on the following day.

Premixed oil-vinegar salad dressing may also be carried in a four-ounce plastic baby bottle. Our former scout troop used larger eight-ounce baby bottles for eight-man patrol salads. Plastic baby bottles seal well and oil will not leak out; plastic jars and water bottles with screw tops are unreliable and generally will leak oil. Undoubtedly some of our success as a backpacking troop had to do with our meals, which could only modestly be described as feasts. Chicken barbequed over a bed of oak coals, hot baking-powder biscuits, salad, and chocolate cakes baked in reflector ovens were not unknown.

One-Pot Suppers (Stews) Are Quick, Tasty, and Easy to Make

Add one can of instant meatballs to the waiting simmering soup stock. Throw in one ounce of dehydrated corn plus one ounce of dehydrated green beans, plus anything else you have left over. Slowly boil about 15 minutes until meat and/or corn is tender. Add a little water if required. Serve in cups. Soak up juice with bread, if you are fortunate enough to have any left. Many similar one-pot meal variations are possible.

The finished one-pot meal described would yield: hot or cold tea, soup, optional salad, and stew. Bread or cookies are generally helpful in soaking up the last traces of stew. Dessert might be accompanied by an after-dinner drink of lemon tea.

Gourmet Two-Pot Suppers

We have very briefly discussed one-pot suppers (essentially stew), which are prepared equally well over one-burner butane stove or wood fire; however, with a wood fire two-pot suppers may be prepared as there is room to simultaneously place two pots over the fire.

Soothing Drink

A good rule to remember at suppertime is that most hikers are pretty tired, so try to get something into them quickly. One simple method is to prepare either hot or cold Start, or Lipton lemon-sugar tea, or Russian tea. Sort of like saying, "We care." After a soothing cup of hot tea everything seems a little brighter and you will be able to think more clearly in the preparation of the gourmet supper to follow.

Soup

Tired hikers need to relax and a slowly consumed supper is actually better for them than a lot of food gulped down quickly. With this thought in mind, the next logical course is a good cup of hot soup. If you are from New York, good soup is chicken noodle soup; other soups are good too. If mushroom soup is on the menu, and is to be used later as gravy, then set aside a cup of soup close to your fire so that it will remain warm.

Meat Entree

Freeze-dried pork chops are an excellent meal, but must first be soaked in an enzyme mix (juice) prepared in your other stainless steel cup. Chops just fit inside the cup. I've never splurged on freeze-dried beef steaks so I don't know if they fit or not. The entire trick in preparing freeze-dried pork chops is to get them to absorb the enzyme juice. I go about this task by turning the chops a few times within the cup of juice so that the bottom chop goes to the top and the top to the bottom. After about three to five minutes of this gentle game, start getting tough and press down hard on the chop with your spoon so that the chop is compressed and then quickly release the spoon pressure to allow the chop to absorb the enzyme juices. Poke and prod and turn and press and repeat, until those blocks of pork slowly become tender all over. When this finally happens you're home free.

Be careful your spoon pressure doesn't cause the chops to scoot out of your cup into the fire or dirt. If this does happen, rinse off your pork chop and try again. If one partner is squeamish about eating pork chops that have bitten the dust, the other overly sympathetic partner will have a true feast. There's a little good in everything.

Fry Pan

The large pot is used as a fry pan, in which successfully soaked chops are placed. Add a trace of water in the pot, in lieu of cooking oil, and brown the chops. Chops will not burn although the meat juice on the pot bottom will burn a little. Do not turn chops too frequently, but from time to time add a trace of water. When chops are browned on both sides you may assume that they are cooked, which in fact they are. At this point you may serve the chops, or go a bit farther down the gourmet trail and simmer them in the mushroom-soup gravy you have saved by the fire.

Cooking Dehydrated Vegetables

While chops are simmering in the mushroom sauce you are busy cooking dehydrated vegetables in the other pot. If you wish to create a third pot where none exists, remove the pork chops and gravy from the cooking pot to your stainless steel cups and set them aside, inside the fire pit to keep them warm. Needless to say, do this carefully. Clean the burned bottom of the pork chop pot and then heat water for dehydrated potatoes or for preparing instant yams, either of which are delicious. Measure potato water accurately, *and if anything a bit on the sparse side,* as you are preparing potatoes, not potato soup. To be sure we are straight on this point, first heat the exact amount of water, then add the potato mix to the pot. If a trace of additional water is needed, use cold water. *Do not* heat water and potato mix together—ugh! This is a common error in camp cooking. Soup you've had; soup you don't want again.

The finished meal described would yield: hot tea, mushroom soup, optional salad, sauteed pork chops in mushroom sauce, potatoes or yams with mushroom gravy, and two vegetables of your choice. If any bread is left you could use it to soak up the gravy. Bread is all gone? Well, "Let them eat cookies!"

Dessert could be a chocolate bar, fruit cookies, instant premixed pudding, cooked fruit, or combinations of pudding and fruit. Being inventive, you'll think of other lightweight delicious combinations. Instant pudding has another basic purpose. Occasionally you'll be so fatigued at the end of the day that you do not wish to eat. Later on you can mix a little pudding with water and slowly sip the dextrose. The energy will help you regain a little of your strength.

After Dinner Drink

What to drink? We have previously discussed hot tea, coffee, chocolate, Start, and Russian tea. You might consider hot liquid Jello, which is sweet, rather thick, and available in different delicate flavors. Or how about an "almost" milkshake on an early-spring backpack. Connie and I mixed instant vanilla pudding, Start orange-drink powder, water, and finally snow, and shook the mixture in our pint plastic water bottle. Not too bad; in fact it was really good. To me the most soothing after-dinner drink is hot Lipton tea with lemon and sugar. Several cups, sipped slowly.

A candy or two saved from your trail food brings a delightful dinner to a happy close, or you may wish to save one piece of candy for a bedtime snack.

After-Dinner Entertainment

After dishes are done (two cups, two spoons, two pots), prepare cooked fruit for breakfast, burn plastic food bags, burn out and flatten tin cans, and suspend food bags and cooked fruit securely from a tree.

This is a good time to fill both water bottles and place them inside your tent. Also fill the one-gallon collapsible water jug so that you will be ready for tomorrow's breakfast. You don't really *need* a collapsible water jug, but its two-ounce weight is made up for many times by its convenience.

Sample Menu for a Four-Day Backpack

	BREAKFAST	LUNCH	SUPPER
FRI.	Sweet rolls, can of apricot juice (eat in car enroute to trailhead)	Trail food (raisins, nuts & M & M's), pepperoni sticks, rye bread, Start orange drink	Potato soup, tuna salad w/ fresh tomato, rye bread, hot tea, chocolate bar
SAT.	Hot Start, cold cereal, with hot milk, rye bread, jam, hot applesauce, hot coffee	Trail food (raisins, nuts & M & M's) chunk of salami, chunk of cheese, rye bread, water (save Start)	Chicken noodle soup, rice with curry, canned baby shrimp, rye bread, cooked peaches, hot coffee

	BREAKFAST	LUNCH	SUPPER
SUN.	Hot Russian tea, scrambled eggs with bacon, toast, jam, hot coffee	Trail food (raisins, nuts & M & M's), canned ham spread, fruit cookies, lemon tea (save raisins)	Mushroom soup, pork chops, gravy, mashed potatoes, green beans and corn, lemon pudding w/raisins, hot Russian tea
MON.	Hot Start, cold cereal with hot milk, fruit cookie, hot coffee	Trail food (raisins, nuts & M & M's), canned liverwurst, fruit cookie, water	Cheeseburger, root beer shake (eat in car enroute home)

It would be wise to include one extra day's food in case you are delayed by bad weather. Food will keep and may be used on another backpack.

Source, Brand Names, Package Weight (Size) of Selected Backpacking Foods to Match Menus

(All quantities are for two people)

BREAKFAST	GROCERY	CAMPING STORE
Orange drink (½ of 4⅝ oz. can)	Start	
Franola cereal (2/3 to 1 cup dry measure)	Pro-Vita	
Hot cereal	X	
Dehydrated milk (2/3 cup dry measure)	Carnation	
Dehydrated apples 3¼ oz. (use ½ package)		King* (REI) Blossom
Dried fruit (2 oz.)	X	

*Recreational Equipment, Inc., Seattle, Washington

108

BREAKFAST	GROCERY	CAMPING STORE
Dehydrated eggs (2 oz. can)		Wilson
Bacon bar (3 oz.)		Wilson
Instant ham (two 1 oz. cans)		Wilson
Instant pork patty (2 oz. can)		Wilson
Jam packets (two ⅝ oz. packets)		X

LUNCH

	GROCERY	CAMPING STORE
Candy, raisins, nuts	X	
Meat sticks, beef, etc.	X	
Hard salami (piece per person)	X	
Hard cheese (piece per person)	X	
Meat spread (4½ oz. can)	Underwood	
Fruit cookies (2 per person)	X	
Crackers, seasoned	Ry-Krisp	
Instant tea (1.8 oz.) (lemon-sugar-Vitamin C ½ packet per 2 servings)	Lipton	

SUPPER

	GROCERY	CAMPING STORE
Dehydrated potato soup (3 oz.)	Lipton	
Dehydrated mushroom soup (2⅜ oz.)		Maggi
Dehydrated vegetable stew mix for salad (2 oz.)		X
Lo-cal salad dressing (1.3 oz., use ½ packet)	Good Seasons	
Canned tuna (6 oz.)	A & P	
Freeze-dried pork chops (2 chops in 2 oz. can)		Wilson
Instant meatballs (1¾ oz. can)		Wilson
Dehydrated potatoes (various flavors) (¼ oz. use 2 packets)	Borden	
Instant yams (3 oz.)		REI
Instant rice	X	
Baby shrimp (5½-6 oz. can)	X	
Curry spices	X	

SUPPER (continued)	GROCERY	CAMPING STORE
Dehydrated vegetables (1 oz.)		REI
Instant pudding (3¾ oz.)	Jello	
Nonmelting chocolate	M & M's	
Nonmelting chocolate bars (two 1 oz. bars)		X

STAPLES

	GROCERY	CAMPING STORE
Bulk instant tea (plain, lemon, sugar, both)	Lipton	
Instant freeze-dried coffee	Maxim	
Sugar, salt, Pream	X	
Snack rye bread (15 oz. loaf)	Gai's	

Fire
Making

Ancient Art

Fire making is an ancient art that has helped man survive and live better through time. Tribes selected their fire makers from responsible men and guardians who passed knowledge down through succeeding generations.

Maintained fires eventually gave way to fire by friction, where heat between rotating spindle and fireboard forms a small growing coal which is cradled in tinder and prayerfully blown into flames. The infant flame is quickly transferred to a prepared pile of tinder and tiny kindling which ignites. Small diameter fuel sticks are carefully added.

One weekend in our basement, in Woodstock, Illinois, my sons and I successfully made fire by friction two or three times in as many hours, using bow, braided leather thong, six-sided rotating wood spindle, and soft, notched fireboard. For us it was hard work and not productive each time. We wore out braided leather thongs, fireboards, spindle, and arm muscles. From time to time we experimented with different woods which didn't materially alter our productivity.

In most cases a coal was formed, but to get that tiny coal to ignite tinder was something else. I have concluded the art is not totally in producing a coal, which is relatively simple, but rather in getting the coal to ignite the tinder. Given this conclusion, I have practiced making a fire in the morning, searching out buried green pea-size coals left over from supper's campfire. Coals are surrounded with tinder and blown into a glowing mass.

111

Two general methods are used to ignite tinder. Tinder may be placed around the coal and blowing takes place at campfire or fireboard level. You'll emerge gray headed with bent back. It is better to lift the tiny coal with your golf ball-size wad of tinder and hold the smoldering wad in your fingers. By compressing the tinder with your fingers while blowing hard on the tinder wad, you can vary tinder density, which I have concluded is also part of the art. The glowing mass will usually ignite, but not always. If it ignites you'll feel a glowing pride. Once tinder is ignited it is treated as if it were a lighted match and quickly placed under a prepared pile of tinder lightly covered with slivers of kindling.

I would not trust my present fire-by-friction skill in the wilderness, as there are too many variables, not the least of which is dry, low density fireboard material, and dry, low-medium density spindle material. This aspect of the art is chancy. Your spindle and fireboard can best be fashioned with a sheath knife, which I no longer carry. Perhaps on a longer wilderness journey one partner *should* carry a sheath knife for serious fire-making duties. Bow and thong are not a problem to obtain (nylon line, braided twisted strips cut from undershirt, bent branch).

Friction by fire is a true primitive art, sometimes managed by one person using bow and thong, but more frequently by two persons taking turns rotating the spindle between the palms of their descending hands, which provide pressure against the fireboard. In either case the action is the same: heat by friction, form a coal, ignite tinder, add fine kindling, and finally, carefully add small-diameter fuel.

Colonists carried flint, steel and tinder in small metal boxes. Woodsmen and Indians used small leather pouches similar to mini shoulder purses. Again: friction causes a spark, charred cloth catches the spark blown into a coal, tinder is ignited, fine kindling added, and finally, fuel of small diameter is carefully added.

With the advent of self-striking matches the ancient art of fire making, or fire starting, became less of a necessity to modern man. He still practiced fire making, but his knowledge of fire starting slowly faded away into history. Self-striking matches require friction, form an instantaneous coal, burst into flames, and the wood match itself ignites supplying initial tinder. If the wood match is the only tinder, it follows that the wood fire must be perfectly prepared for ignition before the match is consumed. This is rare, especially in damp regions of the country.

Good fire making in modern times requires a self-striking match (coal), tinder, kindling and fuel. Times haven't changed that much. Crumpled dry paper, being a thin wood product, performs fairly well as a tinder, but is not always dry or available when needed. If you were separated from your party for the night, and if you carried a wallet on your person, scraps of dry paper in your wallet could be used as tinder. But what if you didn't carry a wallet, or what if the paper burned out before the kindling ignited?

If you are content with making a fire with paper, and if you know you will always have a supply of dry paper available, you may wish to skip the next section on tinder and move on to the kindling section.

Tinder

Tinder is any dry, or essentially dry, wood or weed, in thin or fine pieces, or knife-cut shavings, to which the flame of a wood self-striking match is applied. Good dry tinders burst into flame, damp tinders require more oxygen to burn, so you blow on them. Tinder ignites splintered small-diameter kindling, and kindling, in turn ignites split fuel.

Nothing to it, except, what is tinder?

Two Special Tinders

First, paper-thin sections of birch bark found in the Northwoods which burn dry, damp, or wet due to the volatile oils in the wood cells are an excellent tinder. For fun, locate *downed* birch branches and peel paper-thin bark from the branch. Ignite crumpled piles of birch bark by your campfire and note the quick ignition, sustained burning, and high heat. Half of a hardball-size wad of birch bark will ignite most piles of kindling.

The second-best tinder is dry, long-needled pine needles, which ignite easily as wood cells are filled with resin. Eastern slopes of the Sierra Nevadas and eastern slopes of the Cascade Mountains abound with long-needled pine. Scoop up a handful of needles and needle size pine twigs and light them. Note the quick ignition and high heat. Unlike birch bark, pine needles burn rapidly and require responsive fine kindling.

General Characteristics of Tinder

Other than these two special tinders which vary by region, tinder has certain general characteristics.

1. Tinder is dry; it snaps and crackles when crushed or broken. It is eager to help you, not reluctant. Listen for the sound.

2. Tinder is small in diameter or paper-thin in section, or can be cut and shaved to these sizes with a knife.

3. Tinder is usually dead wood or dead weeds.

4. Wood tinder is usually silver-gray colored. Weed tinder is silver-gray or light beige.

Where to Look for Tinder

Other than special regional tinders previously noted, we are generally looking for dry, dead wood or weeds that snap and crackle when broken. The silver-gray look is a telltale sign and can usually be detected if you look sharply. Silver-colored sumac is an excellent tinder when reduced to shavings. Frequently fallen tree branches will catch on bushes, where they dry in the air. The unnatural angle and silver-gray color are quickly discerned.

114

In the fall, silver-gray weeds are still proudly standing and are usually waiting to be harvested. In the spring silver-gray weeds lie fallen among the green of new growth. Vertical weeds are air dried; horizontal weeds are usually damp and require sun drying or may be air dried on a line or in your tent overnight.

Tinder Sources on Dry Days

On a dry day you can break various weeds and listen to their sound. If they snap and crackle, you've found tinder. Carefully gather very fine-diameter weeds or weed tops and crush them into a loose wad about softball size or larger. You can't have too much, but you can have too little.

Experiment with Local Tinders

Experiment with different weeds and perhaps gather a half dozen varieties. Light them by your campfire and note the desired qualities: instant ignition, high heat, sustained burning, little if any smoke. Make a mental note of the best weed tinder, and in the region you hike use your newly discovered tinder for your next cooking fire and see if it isn't as good or better than paper. Dry weed tinders are gathered in the sunny afternoons and stored overnight in tent pin bags so you'll have dry tinder for breakfast fires. Gather twice as much tinder as required so that if your first fire effort fails, you may try again. Dry leaves and dry grass are generally poor tinders; leaves burn too quickly and have low heat, while grass smokes profusely.

Tinder Sources on Wet Days

On a wet day good dry weed tinders absorb water rapidly and will not snap or crackle when broken or crushed, so they will not be useful if a fire is required immediately. They could be air dried in your tent and might be fine for tomorrow's breakfast fire, but not if you need a fire immediately.

On a damp or rainy day, where do you find dry tinder? Weeds are wet, so narrow your search to wood. There are tricks to finding dry wood on a wet day. Some hints follow.

Reach deep inside, or underneath, downed horizontally splintered trees and break off the dry or driest pieces of wood you can detect. Use your knife and whittle off the damp outer layer of wood. Whittle the dry remainder into a softball-size wad of fine, thin wood shavings. To keep your tinder dry, whittle in your tent, under a rock ledge, or under something. Store whittled dry tinder in your tent or pocket until ready for use.

Reach deep inside old hollow horizontal logs and from the topside break off the dry, thin, flat sections of wood that nature has delaminated for your use. Use your knife, and if wood is damp, whittle away damp layers until a dry layer is located. Whittle dry wood into a softball-size wad of fine, thin wood shavings. Store dry until ready for use. Thin, damp shavings will also burn, reluctantly; you'll need a lot of oxygen and a lot of shavings.

Locate a vertically splintered tree stump with tall fat splinters. Break off a heavy splinter about an arm's thickness or as thick as you can break. Pointed, splintered fragments are excellent as they shed rainwater better than flat stubby ends. Surface of wood is wet *but interior is dry,* so use your knife and whittle off the wet layer, exposing the dry layer underneath, which you will whittle into a softball-size wad of fine, thin wood shavings. Store dry tinder until ready for use.

Lower *dead branches* of pine trees may be split and shaved into tinder in the same manner as fat splinters. Green branches are useless; don't waste your effort.

Kindling

If fine, dry weed tops are good tinder, their lower dry *toothpick-diameter* stalks are good *first-layer* kindling. Also, when shaving wood for tinder, larger shavings too thick for tinder make excellent *first or second layer* kindling.

Small diameter, dead, dry pine branches may be harvested of their *toothpick-diameter* branches for *first-layer* kindling.

Larger dry branches, about pencil diameter, may be split at their forks into two smaller *½ pencil-diameter* pieces of *second-layer* kindling. Reluctant pieces may be split with your pocket knife. Split wood catches fire quicker than whole pieces.

You'll need one handful of first-layer kindling and one handful of second-layer kindling, all about pencil length.

Larger dead split branches, or knife-split dry wood splinters, about *pencil-diameter,* are excellent for *third-layer* kindling. Two handfuls will suffice.

Store dry kindling in a dry place until ready for use.

Fuel

Dead, split (preferably) branches from *finger-thick* diameter up could be regarded as fuel. Cooking fires rarely go beyond finger-sized fuel.

Wet Wood Disaster Fires

Disaster campfires, used to dry out your clothes and body, work best when sustained over a period of several hours. This generally requires larger-diameter wood than may be handled by splitting with a pocket knife or breaking with boots over a rock. Connie and I ended a wet day in an even wetter campsite and had to dry out before bed. We nursed a wet-weather fire into existence, and after one hour reached a point where the fire was capable of sustaining larger pieces of wood. We had been systematically stripping two downed trees of their wood, as described previously, and were down to two- to 3-inch-diameter tree tips.

117

We dragged the two trees over to our fire and placed the tip ends in the flames and coals so that the tips were about two inches apart. As the tips burned away we pulled the trees farther up into the fire. Eventually we had burned the tree down to six- to eight-inch-diameter logs, at which point we were also dry, warm, and ready for bed.

That was a sad night in a way, but an instructive one. We didn't take tent poles in order to reduce pack weight, and used a long splintered stick from a stump as our front tent pole, which of necessity ended up as a roadblock dead center in our doorway. The tent was taut enough, but I don't like my tent exit blocked by a pole. Tents are made for getting in; they are also made for getting out, sometimes quickly.

Our fire-dried hiking socks were overdone on one side, and unlike toast, you can't scrape off the burned part. So the vented pair went into reserve and spare socks were donned. It rained all night, which meant our zippered front door had to be closed, with only four vertical inches left open for ventilation at the tent bottom.

A lonely marmot, or some similar slow-moving animal, insisted on sharing our tent and kept poking his nose into our warm home. I don't blame him; it was a bad night. I didn't take a flashlight or candle, as this particular hike was our "drive-the-weight-down" hike. So we would "shoo!" and close our tent, then gasp for air and open the tent, then mop up rain-driven water, then "shoo!", and so on through the night. (Air will not enter closed tents if sidewalls are sealed by rain, snow, ice or frost. A critical point to remember.)

About 2 A.M. or 3 A.M. Connie became seriously ill. The collective symptoms were those of (1) childbirth, (2) appendicitis, and (3) abdominal witchcraft. We had no light other than matches (and I could not use all of them), no medication other than aspirin, and we were nine trail miles from the last known inhabited camp. The intensity of pain suggested appendicitis; however, the pain was not localized, nor did Connie have a fever. We assumed, or rather hoped, the pain was altitude or food related.

Between groans, rain, nausea, marmot, and believe it or not a stuck tent zipper, our night was an agony. The evening finally ended. Daylight seemed to bring a diluted version of the past evening. After hot tea, all seemed a bit better.

Looking back on this episode, we added flashlight, candle stub, tent poles, and Pepto Bismol tablets to our "necessary" equipment. We also never again bought a "two-man freeze-dried beef stew" packaged in vinyl and foil, as the evidence pointed to undigested pieces of meat that would "reconstitute in 10 minutes." As a safety measure we had boiled that stew, not soaked it, for 20 to 30 minutes, obviously to no avail. Our meat now comes from sealed cans. We pay more, but worry less. One exception is the foil wrapped bacon bar, which has been consistently reliable. One trusted authority uses considerable quantities of meat bar, which apparently is also reliable.

Getting back to "Fuel," we managed to get a wet fire going and sustained it with only a scout knife and a lot of know-how concerning wet fire making. This knowledge is especially useful to backpackers and should be learned and frequently practiced, as it will come in handy on more than one occasion. The object is to survive.

As a complete aside, you haven't lived until you have taken a wet oak branch and whittled tinder, kindling and fuel from this hard wood. In this situation an axe is a prerequisite.

Building a Fire

Carefully place, don't throw, each piece of tinder, kindling and fuel so that you do not topple the fire structure you are building. Making a fire in the rain requires a sheltered location or a protective overhead canopy such as a large, flat rock or pack. One raindrop can negate all your previous skilled efforts. Once a fire is burning strongly, a light rain doesn't seem to bother it. In a strong rain a small tarp is essential. In scouting, each patrol carried a tarp for eight-man

BUILDING A FIRE

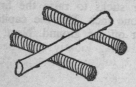

1. Make an "H" with the crossbar off the ground.

2. Add tinder. Add tooth pick size sticks in teepee fashion.

Tinder

3. Same as 2. Add larger pieces to teepee. Make three teepee layers in all.

4. Form a log cabin around the teepee. Add a roof

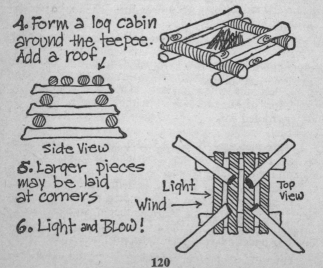

Side View

5. Larger pieces may be laid at corners

Light

Wind

Top View

6. Light and BLOW!

patrol cooking. Connie and I do not carry a small tarp; perhaps we should.

To light a fire the match must be held *under* the tinder, so I place a finger-size stick on top of and perpendicular to two similar sticks to raise the first stick off the ground about one inch, like the capital letter "H," with the crossbar off the ground. Next, I place pencil-size pieces of kindling loosely (air space between) across the first stick to form a small lean-to. On top of the lean-to I place half of my tinder, saving the other half in case the first fire-making effort fails. This lean-to provides room to get my lighted match *under* the tinder.

Over the tinder I loosely arrange half of the first layer *toothpick-diameter* kindling, in a flat teepee design pressed close to the tinder. Save the other half of the first-layer kindling.

Over the first-layer kindling I loosely place half of the second layer, *½ pencil-diameter* kindling in a slightly higher teepee design, sort of a teepee over a teepee, yet intimate with the first teepee. Save the other half of the second-layer kindling. Over the second-layer kindling I loosely place half of the third layer *pencil-diameter* kindling, a teepee over two teepees, loose yet again intimate. Save the other half of the third layer of kindling.

Half of the split fuel is placed log cabin style around the kindling teepee. Two small pieces of split fuel are placed one way, crossed by two small pieces of split fuel placed the other way, etc. The shape of the log cabin sort of hugs the teepee within. The log cabin is loosely roofed with split fuel. Save the other half of the split fuel.

Larger pieces of fuel are laid teepee style over the crossed corners of the log cabin and then teepee style around the entire log cabin.

The step-by-step procedure is deliberate, yet certain. It will produce a fire from one match just about every time. Once material has been gathered and prepared, the actual fire building takes about one minute. Fire building under adverse conditions *must be certain.*

Lighting a Fire

Hopefully you have left an opening in your fire structure for lighting the tinder. Have a stone handy on which to strike your match. You and your partner huddle together to block the wind by opening your rain jackets to form an effective windscreen, *blocking the wind which is at your back,* if you have properly oriented your fire.

Strike your match as close as possible to the prepared fire. Tilt the head of the wood match down so that the flame runs up the wood match, and, once burning, quickly hold the lighted match *under the lean-to* so the flame will burn up through the tinder above. Be careful not to ram the lighted match into stick, earth, or lean-to, which will extinguish your match. This is a common problem and it could be your last match. Hold match steady and wait a second, until you are certain tinder is burning, before dropping match. Sometimes I hold a piece of thin kindling in with the match to prolong the burning under the tinder. Dry-wood fires will roar away when exposed to match. Dry-wood fires are easy to start.

Starting Damp-Wood Fires

Now, if tinder and the entire edifice was whittled from damp wood, it will take a little longer for the tinder to ignite. In this case cut off a half inch from the wick end of your candle stub and place it under the lean-to, then light the candle, which will burn longer than the match and permit the tinder to dry out a bit from the heat of the prolonged candle flame. This "fire starter" is the second reason you have toted the half ounce of candle stub on each and every hike.

Damp-wood fires require a lot of tinder and a lot of tiny kindling to develop a self-drying out operation. Damp-wood fires also require a lot of oxygen; gentle blowing on ignited tinder, and harder blowing on kindling. Blowing consumes tinder and kindling rapidly, so have a good supply on hand. Blowing also exhausts people, so rotate the chore frequently.

I do not add fuel to damp-wood fires until the burning kindling base has been well established. Damp-wood fires require nursing for an hour, sometimes all the time—they are delicately started and should never be presumed to be okay. Stay on them with oxygen and add kindling as necessary. When blowing on a fire, get down low to the ground and attempt to *blow under and up the fire,* rather than down, which puts the fire out.

Slowly change to larger pieces of fuel, always being sure the *base of kindling is burning well.* Be careful not to smother the fire. Wood is always laid loosely, meaning with air space between pieces.

Maintaining Fires

Many fires fail because the inside burns up before the outside catches fire. This suggests that a lot of tinder and fine kindling are required. Most people do not use enough; conversely, most people add too many large pieces and add them too quickly. It is advisable to slip in a few finer pieces to feed the inside of the fire when adding thicker pieces to feed the outside of the fire. One for the inside and one for the outside, etc.

Likewise, when logs of larger diameter, four to six inches, are dragged over a fire, be sure to keep the fire bed burning by adding smaller pieces of fuel between the logs. Larger logs should always be placed and burned in pairs; lonesome logs do not burn well, a most useful fact as we shall see.

Extinguishing Fires

If water is not available, or cannot be spared, pull larger logs out of the fire and rub them into the soil to extinguish all glowing areas. Rub one log against another to get at deep seated glowing areas. Beat one log against the other to detect and dislodge sparks. Do this with all larger pieces of burning wood until only the bed of coals remains to be extinguished. Spread coals thinly and rub them into the soil, using a stick. Do one area at a time and work to the center, where the fire was the hottest. Repeat the process until all coals are out. Overturn fireplace rocks and get at all concealed coals. Leave all large pieces burned wood separated and alone so they don't start up a warm friendship.

If water is available, drown the fire, embers, large logs and soil. Stir drowned coals with a stick. Overturn fireplace rocks and drown under and between them. Some hot rocks explode when water hits them, so proceed with caution. I have heard this advice all my life and have yet to meet an exploding rock; however, it is technically possible.

In both the soil and water methods of extinguishing fires, pick out all trash, wire ties, aluminum foil, unburned garbage, etc. and place it in a plastic bag and pack it out. When the fire is totally out, roll fireplace and fire-ring stones over the fire area to constrain it if for some strange reason it gets started again.

Fires must be totally extinguished for very selfish reasons: you and your partner could easily become trapped by a rapidly spreading forest fire, and even if you weren't injured, your favorite campsite would be destroyed for many years to come. It is very educational to hike deliberately through a burned-out forest. Our family did this once in the Mt. Baker National Forest and the total devastation was spooky. Very similar to flattened, bombed-out villages I saw in Germany during World War II.

First-Aid
Supplies

Carry Knowledge and Supplies

Our small bag of first-aid supplies (eight ounces) is stocked to relieve minor problems and take the pain out of major ones. We carry a lot of boy scout and Red Cross first-aid knowledge, but few supplies.

I suggest you carry a one-ounce pamphlet on mountain medicine or a similar booklet in your first-aid bag. (See section on Reference Books.)

Pills

You've heard the story of Connie's violent reaction to some dehydrated beef stew. No medication was available, nor did we have a flashlight or candle to provide at least a little cheer on a cheerless night. We now carry one tiny flashlight with one alkaline battery and twelve Pepto Bismol tablets. Both are effective. We also carry about twelve aspirin tablets in a small plastic bag to relieve minor pain.

Tape and Tablets

Adhesive tape is easily carried by discarding the metal spool and cover and wrapping the five yards of half-inch-wide tape around the small plastic vial containing 20 salt tablets. Salt tablets help overcome heat exhaustion in hot uphill hikes and adhesive tape is useful for preventing "hot spots" on your heels from developing into blisters on uphill hikes, or on your toes on downhill hikes.

Cuts and Worse

For small cuts, we carry six bandaids. We prefer cotton adhesive cloth, as it seems more reliable than plastic tape, which frequently doesn't stick. For larger cuts, adhesive tape "butterflies" may be cut from the adhesive tape with your scout knife. In applying pressure directly over a larger cut, four wrapped sterile three-inch-square compresses could be helpful. Bandages to hold compresses in place may be fashioned from your bandana or from strips cut from a cotton T-shirt and secured by some of the 12 safety pins carried.

Sprains or Worse

Ankle bandage for a twisted ankle or an arm sling could also be fashioned from a bandana or T-shirt. (See *Boy Scout Handbook* in Reference Books section.)

Infection and Pain Killers

One half-ounce tube of antibacterial ointment helps prevent possible infection from minor cuts. Our physician prescribed twelve penicillin tablets which we carry in case of potential infection that the ointment cannot handle. He also prescribed twelve pain-killing pills for major painful emergencies.

Once in the Tetons I developed an infected toe about midway on a six-day backpack. It was very reassuring to have penicillin. On another occasion Hazen Arnold, an explorer scout now living in Ohio, severely smashed his finger under a heavy rock, which showed us that our habit of carrying pain pills was an excellent one. Our backpacking average over the last ten years was one usage of pain pills and two usages of penicillin —safer than at home, where over the same period of time we have had a total of eight severe twists, breaks and slashes. Skiing and football were the major contributors. Incidentally, both infected-toe patient and smashed-finger patient recovered, although one now has a wider finger.

Digging and Sewing

With our first-aid bag we also carry two feet of rip-stop red nylon tape to repair bags or jackets, two needles for removing splinters and sewing chores, and one spool of heavy thread for repairing clothing, tents, bags or packs. Only once did we have a tent flap rip in a high wind, but we were able to sew a patch to keep the ripped flap from spreading and further damaging our tent. It was our own fault; we didn't properly close the flap on our four-person tent. Obviously you can't carry first-aid supplies for every emergency, but you can be prepared for major and minor common problems, such as have been described.

Tranquilizer

A two-ounce plastic bottle of mosquito repellent, available from REI for 39¢, is suggested to restore tranquility as you hike, or in camp areas infected by the persistent little devils. One of my "pro" backpacking friends tells me the ingredient to look for is N, N-DIETHYL-META-TOLUAMIDE (whatever that is). The REI brand, known simply as "insect repellent" has 71.25% of this bug-chasing ingredient. Really works. Mosquitoes hover near your skin, but will not alight, much less sting. Read "caution" on the label carefully.

Prevent Burns

The kitchen is the most dangerous place in home and camp. Boiling pots of water are not always needed; use hot water in lieu of boiling water to reduce the danger of scalding. Boiling pots of food can spill, so hold the pot bail handle while you stir. Hot bail handles can sear your fingers, so use your bandana-pot holder. The butane stove's hot grill can burn your fingers if you pick up the stove's grill before it's cool.

The stove or campfire can ignite your hair as you bend over to light the stove or blow on the campfire to get it started. Any fire can ignite your clothing, tent, pack, or burn up your food supply. Sparks will smolder on cotton and burn neat holes through nylon. Dry-season camping is a good time to forgo the pleasure of a wood cooking fire and rely solely on your butane stove.

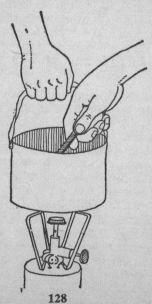

Prevent Cuts

Cuts generally occur when a knife is used in preparing food. Avoid sudden movements when cutting. Pocket knives can snap shut on fingers. I used to carry a sheath knife almost exclusively to prepare tinder and kindling for a fire, but I no longer carry one after it cut through the sheath and was waving around waiting for me to slash myself. Sadly, that sheath knife is now retired.

Opened tin cans have sharp edges and sharper lids. Burned-out cans should be allowed to cool before flattening them to avoid possible contact with fingers.

Prevent Slashes

Don't worry one second about axe cuts or dismemberments because you *do not need, nor will you be carrying,* an axe. Forget it! If you haven't got it you can't destroy yourself with it. Few people have the foggiest notion of how to cut with an axe. In scouting, it took about one year for scouts to develop expertise; I wouldn't attempt to convey the required skill and proper attitude in a section within a chapter of a book. If you can't break a stick with your boot, the stick is too large; go find a smaller one. Little sticks are best for cooking; big logs are sawed and axe split for your fireplace at home, not in camp, and most certainly not on a backpack.

Prevent Blisters

The subject is still accident prevention, and since you are hiking, going uphill may blister your heel, while going downhill may blister the tops of your toes. Generally, walking flat-footed going uphill, and tightening your boot laces a bit going downhill will prevent blisters. When faced with the prospect of hours of continuous downhill travel it might be wise to consider wearing two pairs of socks. Two pairs seem to plug up the void in the toe space so that your toes are cushioned as the downhill angle rams your toes forward in the boot.

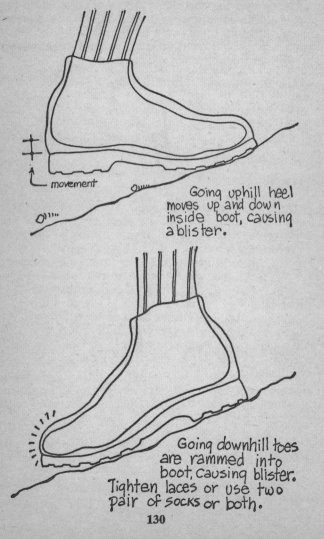

movement

Going uphill heel moves up and down inside boot, causing a blister.

Going downhill toes are rammed into boot, causing blister. Tighten laces or use two pair of socks or both.

130

You can usually detect a "hot spot" (blister about to happen) on your heel or toe, and when pain *first alerts you,* stop and apply half-inch-wide adhesive tape directly to the "hot spot" before a blister develops. On heels, use overlapping horizontal strips, with one vertical strip over the horizontal strips and centered on the tendon. This covering resembles a lap siding on a house and will absorb some of the boot friction. While it may not keep a blister from developing, it will usually keep the blister from breaking and bleeding.

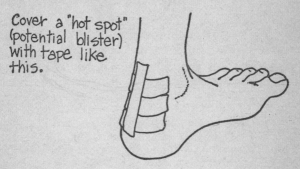

Cover a "hot spot" (potential blister) with tape like this.

Prevent Twisted Ankles

What easier way to injure yourself than by twisting your ankle on the trail? It just takes a second to stumble over a rock or root or to actually step right off the edge of a high-angle trail. Watch where you walk. Sounds trite, but really, watch where you step, as a twisted ankle can be a pain to all concerned. The entire party would be handicapped, or rather pedicapped. Every scout knows to step over, not upon, objects on the trail. Now you also know. Be cautious crossing small streams on wet peeled logs.

Prevent Falls

Slow down when going downhill to avoid stumbling. If you slip on a high-angle traverse across a grassy meadow, don't fight it; immediately sit down and start grabbing bushes, grass, moss or dirt. Grab something! Walk, don't run while on trail or in camp. On a steep trail a fall will put you into orbit. In camp, a fall will usually be over a tent guyline. If you try hard enough you'll fall down and knock over the pot of food; in that manner you can go to bed bruised, burned, and hungry, sharing your tent with your hungry, disbelieving partner; "I can't believe you spilled the whole thing!"

Prevent Cut Feet

Wear shoes as you walk in camp. No need to take them off, merely loosen the laces. Bare feet are no match for sharp rocks or roots. I know of one young man who required six stitches to close up the gash between his toes just because he liked to walk barefoot in camp. Take care of your feet, as they are your only means of transportation back home. Better to read about it here than bleed in camp. At Northwoods Scout Camp near Boulder Junction, Wisconsin, they have a sensible rule: "Wear your boots all the time, except when swimming and sleeping."

Prevent Sunburn

Wearing a shirt or a T-shirt will avoid sunburn. If you must get sunburned, don't injure your feet, shoulders, back and thighs, in that order.

Prevent Becoming Chilled

When taking a brief rest, or when eating lunch along the trail, put on your down jacket to avoid becoming chilled. The main idea is to put on additional clothing *before you become chilled,* as it may take hours to warm up once you are chilled. Head colds and flu seem to have some relationship to rapidly changing body temperature, so avoid a chill. The chill concept is most pronounced in the evening at suppertime. Enjoy your supper; however, if you become even slightly chilled, slip on a sweater or down jacket, as night temperatures fall quickly in the mountains, and you'll never get warmer, only colder.

Prevent Ear Ache

On one hike the wind bothered my ear until I tore tiny strips of cloth out of my bandana and made ear plugs, which cured the situation right away. A lightweight bandana hat will also cover your head in wind or intense sun. My sons and I piled snow on our heads in the Tetons to keep our bandana hats damp in the 80-degree heat.

Wear Sunglasses

On one snowhike I forgot my polarized sunglasses, and within a few hours I began to see pink spots everywhere I looked. Luckily we left the snow area before further damage or pain occurred.

Sleep Dry and Warm

My former scout troop developed the habit of telling stories in the evening while sitting around a fire drying out damp clothing before going to bed. We did this particularly on winter camps, but the technique is valid in the summer in the mountains. It's a good idea to slow down in the evening and dry out by a fire if possible. If for any reason your clothing is wet or damp from sweat, and you can't dry out by a fire, change into dry clothing before going to bed. In any event, at least put on dry socks before going to bed. Dry clothing is significantly warmer than damp clothing.

Avoid Becoming a Statistic

Avoid campsites that could harm you, such as dead overhanging branches waiting to fall down on you. Trees are very impartial and a dead tree could just as well fall on you as not. The tree will fall over sometime, so why take chances and camp within its reach?

You wouldn't camp under poised, waiting boulders, as they too have to fall sometime. Notice all the boulders around your intended campsite. Ask yourself, "Where did all these boulders come from?" Find a better campsite; who needs a rolling tombstone?

Dry riverbeds or camps close to a riverbank may be freely assumed to flood on the night you camp there. Why ask for it? Have an awareness of other campers' locations, Ranger stations (radio), manned lookout towers (radio), airfields (radio), and villages (radio or phone) that may be near your route.

Avoid Being Crushed

If a horse or mule train approaches, get uphill on the trail so the animals won't crush or kick you. One authority suggests you talk to the animals so they know you are human. I suppose that's okay, depending on what you say and on how well the animal understands.

Avoid Falling off a Cliff

Backpacking is fun for kids too, but do not let them run ahead alone out of sight, as many trails split into two trails and almost all trails have steep drop offs somewhere along the route. It's the nature of trails. A distant relative by marriage lost his young son over a cliff. Apparently the boy ran ahead to "hide," and ran behind a rock on the edge of a 150-foot cliff, where he fell to his death. He wasn't found by mountain rescue teams until two days after he dropped out of sight.

On the "main highway" from Canyon Creek to Miners Ridge (Glacier Peak area, Washington), there is a concealed 85-degree drop off on the edge of the trail that falls 20 feet to the first bump and then drops straight down about 50 feet to the second bump. Hundreds of people walk within one foot of that point each year. The potential fall is probably fatal. I wonder how many hikers are aware of the danger?

Avoid Smashing Your Body

Under the ongoing discussion of accident prevention, we should include glissading. Select a slope with a safe runout (e.g., no cliffs or boulders at the bottom). The best way to determine whether or not a slope is safe is to walk up the edge of the snowfield and observe your intended ski route. Also be sure there are no protruding rocks to slice into you. Glissading is a lot of fun, but do it intelligently, as it happens to be the cause of the second greatest number of accidents in rock and snow climbing. The most frequent cause is rapelling. Both are simple, both are downhill, a combination that apparently causes even experienced people to abandon caution.

Learn Basic First Aid

Our book will not attempt to get into bandages, slings, splints, or carries, as these subjects are covered in varying depth in other recognized journals. If you are a young person, you would do well to join the boy scouts or girl scouts or explorer scouts (for young men and women), as it is excellent basic training for camping, canoeing and backpacking. The basic subject of First Aid is handled well by most troops and some posts and will be remembered all your life. If you are an adult you might consider enrolling in one of the Red Cross first-aid courses offered in industry or at most colleges in the physical-education department.

Among the scouts in my former troop, Pat Pajac saved his friend, Bob Davis, from possible death by promptly stopping serious arterial bleeding. If Pat had run to get help, as many untrained people do, his friend would have bled to death. I personally witnessed one small child saved from drowning by sons Chuck and Tom at White Pines State Park, near Oregon, Illinois.

Summary of First-Aid Supplies Carried in First-Aid Bag for Two People for Two Days to Two Weeks

 1 Mountaineering medicine booklet
 8 Pepto Bismol tablets
12 Aspirin tablets
20 Salt tablets
12 1-inch Safety pins
 5 yards ½-inch Adhesive tape
 1 ½-oz. Tube antibacterial ointment
 1 2-oz. Plastic bottle mosquito repellent
 6 Bandaids
 4 3-inch Sterile compress
 2 Heavy needles
 1 Spool coat thread
 2 ft. Nylon mending tape
*12 Penicillin tablets
*12 Pain tablets

Bandages may be fashioned from your bandana or from strips cut from your T-shirt. A tiny flashlight helps to find medication you may need during the night.

For your own personal confidence on and off the trail, I strongly suggest you purchase a *Boy Scout Handbook,* or *First Aid Merit Badge* pamphlet, and that you at least understand and become proficient in:

(1) direct pressure to stop bleeding
(2) mouth to mouth resuscitation

*Type and strength by doctor's prescription

(3) treatment for shock

(1) ankle bandage tied over a boot.

Knowledge doesn't cause accidents, it helps to prevent them, and if they do happen, helps to increase your chances of coming out smiling, or at least coming out.

It's an old adage, but don't knock it: "Be prepared."

Sleeping and Housekeeping

Share Duties

In the mountains night temperatures drop rapidly and wind velocity increases, which hastens most fatigued backpackers into their windfree tents and warm mummy bags. Darkness comes quietly and quickly as peaks surrender their light to ascending night. If you are going to bed at sunset it follows that during daylight hours all has been made ready for sleeping. A simple division of tasks is to have one partner cook supper while the other partner pitches the tent and arranges gear within the tent.

Both backpackers should share equally in eating and dishwashing, although there is historical precedence to suggest a burned pot is cleaned by the cook, who correspondingly has the pleasant privilege, but not the obligation, of licking good pots clean.

Gather Wood

If you plan on a wood fire for cooking breakfast, it would be wise to gather tinder and kindling while there is still light to see what you are doing. Store dry fire-making materials in your tent pin bag inside your tent for the night so dew or rain will not dampen them. If you plan on a wood fire for cooking supper, and perhaps for dreaming around after supper, you would do well to gather wood during daylight, as you will not be able to see downed wood in the dark.

Preparing Beds

The noncooking partner pitches the tent as described earlier. Foam pads are placed in the tent first, with odds and ends placed under the head end of the pad to help contribute to a "pillow." Tent pin bags, tent pole bags, and 15-foot coil of nylon line used to tie the foam pads all become "pillow" material.

Next, unroll mummy bags, fluff them up, and place stuff sack under foam pad for additional "pillow." Generally bags are placed with zippers facing one another, which is friendly and suggests that hikers have a preference for sleeping on one side or the other. This results in a "right" and "left" to the tent which is quickly settled by asking who wants to sleep on which side. Beats sleeping with your nose against the cold tent sidewall.

Pillow and Slope Adjuster

Plastic-wrapped spare-clothing bag is placed on top of the foam pad to act as a true pillow. Fold your down jacket on top of the clothing bag and you will have a superb pillow. If additional pillow height is needed, an empty pack may be folded and placed under the foam pad. This is also handy for raising the head end of the foam pad if the campsite slopes down at the head end of the tent. By varying the amount of pillow material you will be able to suit personal taste and accommodate varying hillside slopes.

Water Bottles and Breakfast

Both filled water bottles are placed at the head end of the tent, where they will be handy if you need a drink during the night. First-aid bag is placed near the water bottles so aspirin and Pepto Bismol are also handy, should the need arise.

If chipmunks are not seen in your camp area tomorrow morning's breakfast bag and spoons may be placed inside the two nesting cooking pots. If chipmunks are present, *all food* should be suspended from a tree. Match-safe, scout knife, tiny flashlight and candle stub are placed inside the nested cups.

SLEEPING

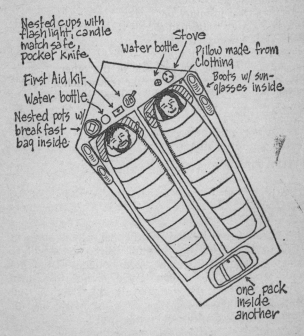

Nested cups with flash light, candle match safe, pocket knife

First Aid Kit
Water bottle
Nested pots w/ breakfast bag inside →

Water bottle
Stove
Pillow made from clothing
Boots w/ sun-glasses inside

one pack inside another

Note: Under pads are: 15' lines, pole bag, pinbag, stuff sack, bandana. Tinder & kindling for breakfast fire in pinbag or stuff sack. Food is hung up outside in net bag from 50' line. Hikers wearing: socks, under-wear, trousers, orlon sweater (cool weather). Packs could go under pad as extra pillow if head sloping down hill.

Wedges

Your unzipped rain jacket can be opened to its fullest width and roughly folded about one foot wide and placed lengthwise between your mummy bag and tent sidewall. In case of a hard-driving rain on your side of the tent, it just might keep seam seepage off your sleeping bag. If your tentsite slopes down on your side of the tent, your rain jacket may be used as a wedge to more or less level your pad.

Boots are taken off *before* you enter the tent and banged together to knock off any mud stuck between the cleats. Stand on the floored vestibule during this operation, then back directly into your sleeping bag. Boots are placed between the small of your back and the tent sidewall, or in the space at the head of your tent, or they may be used as a wedge under your foam pad to aid in making a pillow, or to help level a badly sloping tentsite.

To Bed

It seems to me we have fairly well set the stage for your tired, well-fed body to fall asleep. You will recall from our previously described clothing list that you are not backpacking pajamas; you do not need them.

If the temperature is extremely hot, sleep in your dry underclothes on top of your mummy bag. As the night becomes cooler your body will be the first to know and you can slip inside your sleeping bag.

If the temperature is moderate, sleep inside your mummy bag wearing only dry underclothes. You might begin the night with your bag unzipped and close it up as the cool night air makes known its presence.

If the temperature is cool, sleep with your orlon long-sleeve sweater next to your bare skin, wear a pair of dry socks, and you'll probably want to sleep in your dry trousers.

If the temperature is cold, or turns cold, take your down jacket off your pillow and wear it over your Orlon sweater inside your mummy bag. As the temperature gets even colder tighten up the drawstring on your mummy-bag hood so that only your nose is outside. If it gets even colder, sleep back-to-back with your partner, as the small of the back seems to be another critical cold spot and body heat will keep it warm.

Tent Ventilation

Usually you'll want your mosquito netting closed and your tent flaps open to watch the departing day and emerging stars. On a really cold night or in high winds partially close down the tent flap opening, which will warm the tent a few degrees above outside temperature. In a front-driving rain close the flaps almost completely, leaving only a few inches open for ventilation. Generally try to keep the flaps open or partially open so you can breathe the fresh mountain air rather than your own products of combustion.

In snow or frost areas the tent must be vented in the event that snow, ice or frost should seal the fabric outside or inside and deplete oxygen required for breathing. I would not begin to recommend a "tent heater," as I can still recall reading about two hunters in Illinois who died in their truck camper as a result of a "tent heater" consuming oxygen. Connie and I have always left our tent flaps fully or partially opened in all types of weather. I would like to modify our tent with a hooded, vented, screened opening above the door, which would be particularly helpful in a frontal rain. I hesitate to mention some of my "fantastic" ideas to Connie, as it usually means she and her sewing machine have to get busy. I think I'll play it safe and not say anything.

Tent Functions

Tents primarily shield you from heat-robbing wind, rain and mosquitos; tents do not in themselves produce heat. Your body produces heat from the food you've eaten at supper. Your dry clothing and dry mummy bag insulate and conserve body-generated heat.

Rainstorms

Occasionally you'll encounter a wind or rainstorm that sounds and feels as if it will blow your tent right off your campsite. At times like that you'll be awake anyway and instead of lying quietly in pure terror so as not to wake your partner, who is lying quietly in pure terror so as to not wake you, you might break the apprehension with sure-fire remarks like, "Sounds like it's beginning to rain!"

Man the Bilge Pumps

Usually it is reassuring to switch on your tiny flashlight and look for leaks and puddles. Check to be sure your spare-clothing bag is still on top of your foam pad and that all of your clothes are still inside the plastic bag. Probably a few puddles will be on the vestibule floor, where wind-driven rain penetrated the flap zipper or entered through the partially open flap. Use your bandana to mop up the puddles and wring out the water inside a cooking pot. When water is mopped up empty the pot outside the tent.

This is an excellent time to light the candle stub, as nothing is quite as cheery as candlelight. Turn one cup upside down and stick the candle to it with a drop of melted wax. Be careful that the flame is away from your hair and tent fabric. Candles add a bit of heat to a tent, although the major benefit may be more psychological than physical. After a few minutes, when you and your partner are both satisfied that you are alive, well, and haven't floated away, you can blow out the candle and attempt to get back to sleep.

The Longest Night

Some nights are longer than others, and if this is one of them, be patient. Everything seems a little better when daylight eventually appears. One fun topic on nights that are pure disaster is to discuss favorite foods in detail. It is difficult to be apprehensive when mentally preparing and eating your favorite food or slowly sipping your favorite drink.

Breakfast in Bed

Eventually morning arrives and when you can see what you are doing, it is fun to have breakfast in bed. Since you have stove, pots, cups, spoons, water and breakfast-food bag, you might as well make a little room in the vestibule of the tent and prepare breakfast.

Be sure to vent the tent a little if you decide to use your butane stove. Obviously the stove must be stable and you'll remember to hold the bail handle on the pot while your partner stirs. Normally you'll be heating water, not boiling it, for hot drinks or for hot milk for

145

your cereal; in this manner if the pot did spill, you would not be scalded. Stove heat will warm your tent and the food will warm your body and spirit. Mountain storms have a way of letting up in the morning, so with any luck when breakfast is over the storm may be also.

Assuming it is still raining after breakfast, you might as well wash your spoon, cup and pots by placing them outside the tent and finger-wiping them. Once dishes are done you may wish to leave the pots outside to collect drinking water to refill water bottles.

Singing in the Rain

On rainy days you have two choices: spend the day in your tent, or hike out in the rain to your next campsite.

If you elect to stay in your tent your two biggest chores will be: retrieve your food bag tied up in a tree, and go to the bathroom.

Let's assume you have elected to pack up and hike out. Your four biggest chores then will be: retrieve your food bag tied up in a tree, go to the bathroom, pack up all your belongings while you and your partner are both inside the tent, and step outside into the cold wet world to take down your faithful tent.

Packing Up Inside Tent

Packing up inside a tiny two-person mountain tent during a rain is somewhat hilarious and really needs a word or two of explanation. This is one of those moments when all the philosophy of lightweight backpacking comes home to roost. The less you have the easier it will be to pack. The real key is merely to have only one person work at a time. (E.g., one partner rolls and compresses his mummy bag while the other partner offers advice and comfort; when one bag is done then it is the other partner's turn.) Likewise, only one person can struggle to get dressed while lying horizontally in a narrow, low-roofed tent. Some packing can be done simultaneously, but generally it is difficult for two people to thrash around inside a small tent at the same time.

Both packs are completely assembled inside the tent, and both partners are completely dressed before they step outside to take down the tent. You have set aside the 50 feet of ⅛-inch nylon line, pin bag and pole bag. Ready? Let's go!

Packing a Wet Tent

With the tent up, quickly shake off all the water you can, as wet tents are many times heavier than dry tents. Quickly pull pins, disassemble poles and place them in their bags within the pack. Both partners compress the ballooning tent to expel the air trapped inside. Guy-lines are placed on top of the tent.

With a certain amount of moaning and groaning, the sopping tent will be rolled lengthwise and lashed horseshoe style around the outside of your pack. In fairness to the poor soul packing the heavy wet tent, the other partner should carry the pins and poles, plus a little additional load, perhaps the butane stove and spare fuel cartridge. This small gesture will go a long way to soothe the feelings of the wet-tent carrier.

Take All Your Belongings

In your haste to leave be sure to take down the soaked socks hanging on the line, or more probably, blown downwind from the line. Occasionally a wallet will slide out of the tent as it is being folded. In short, be sure to leave with all your belongings, wet or otherwise. One authority suggests red clothing, as it is easy to spot in the green, brown, white and blue world of wilderness.

You may note, with some degree of confidence for future camps, that the area underneath your tent was dry.

Try Again

You survived the night; in fact, you handled a rather difficult situation fairly well. Bask in your glory as you slosh along to your next campsite. As soon as you get there, dry out everything that is wet by a fire, assuming the rain has stopped. If the rain hasn't stopped, treat yourself to the best high-energy supper you can put together inside your wet world. Ironically this tough night will be remembered long after easy camps are forgotten. If it helps any, remember that your spare clothes are dry, assuming that you didn't wash them at your last camp, leaving them still wet or damp. If they are still wet or damp you may be in serious trouble.

Camp and Trail Sanitation

Bend a Little

When arriving at your campsite for the evening, pick up and burn debris left by thoughtless people. When leaving camp go over the entire area and pick up all debris left by anyone. If everyone picked up his own and others' debris, our wilderness would remain forever beautiful. If we start today there will be less for all of us to pick up tomorrow.

Coca Cola featured a charming young lady in one of its ads bending down to pick up litter. The caption read, "Bend a little." Rather clever, as some people will not lower themselves to pick up their own trash, let alone someone else's trash. Actually it's a mental attitude; if you "bend" mentally, the physical bend is easy. Picking up your campsite flatters your ego, as you have demonstrated you are a "good" guy. Hopefully all backpackers will become "good" guys; it could become contagious. Over a period of time the alternative is to camp in state and national garbage dumps.

Dishwashing

Lightweight backpacking is a dishwasher's paradise. Responsibility boils down to each person cleaning his own cup and spoon. The cook cleans the cooking pots. (You burn 'em, you clean 'em.)

Dishwashing is done in a cooking pot, not in streams or lakes, and is done away from streams, lakes, trails, and campsites.

Liquid garbage and dirty dishwater should be poured into an out-of-the-way hole in the ground or deep under bushes that are well away from campsite, trail, stream, or lake.

Never wash dirty dishes or pots directly in a stream, as you are contributing to fouling the water supply of fellow hikers camping downstream. Take water from a stream, but wash and dispose of the used water elsewhere. The only dishes that go into a stream are your clean cup when you want a drink, your clean cooking pot when you are hauling water, and your water bottles when you are filling them.

Unfortunately, we have all inherited camps where dishwater was thrown all over the campsite. This ugly practice is analogous to neighbors slopping dishwater over the carpet in your home. I regard the fragile flowers, moss and struggling grass as my carpet when out camping and try to do them the least harm possible.

Blue Monday

Most folks rinse out rather than wash clothing; however, if you are compulsive soaper, pack a sliver of soap for the one or two times you will be washing underclothes, socks, etc. Rinsing or washing is fine if on your laundry day in camp the sun is out and a wind air dries your wet clothes, but be cautious not to end up with damp or wet clothing just before a cold or wet spell sets in. Better dry and dirty than wet and clean. Wet clothing strung out on top of your pack as you hike along dusty trails picks up dust and becomes dirtier than it was before you washed it.

If you must tote washed, wet, heavy clothes, place them inside a plastic bag so that they will not wet other items of clothing or food. Hang them on a bush to dry at lunch breaks and later, when you get into camp, set up a clothesline.

Better yet, don't wash clothes before hiking unless weather is absolutely in your favor.

Polar Bear Club

Try and rinse off your sweaty, dusty body every day or so in lakes or streams. Don't use soap as it may contaminate the water you will be drinking downstream.

Bathing in icy mountain lakes or streams is a fleeting experience accompanied by fierce determined facial expressions, guttural warlike sounds, howls of agony, with dripping iced bodies flashing toward shore like corks popping up and out of the water. I swear some people never touch the surface as they race across the ice water toward shore.

If you can't get up enough nerve to totally immerse yourself in the ice water, at least rinse your hot feet and dusty legs as best you can. Most backpacking people understand your needs, so don't be unduly bashful.

Burn Solid Garbage and Pack Out Cans

Solid garbage, such as leftover food, should be burned a little at a time over a small hot fire; if you put too much garbage on the fire at one time you may smother the fire, so add a little at a time. Nothing smells quite as bad as burning garbage, so wait until meals are finished before going into the garbage business. Plastic bags, aluminum foil envelopes, and cans are burned out over your fire. When the fire is out, aluminum foil is picked out of the fire and placed inside burned-out cans, which are then flattened with boot heel or rock and packed out.

The logic in this case is that if you are able to carry heavy full cans in, you are more than able to carry light empty cans out. If you save one of the large plastic food bags, the aluminum and flattened cans will have a home and will not dirty the inside of your pack.

Toilets

Simple toilets, located well off the trail and away from streams, lakes and campsites may take several forms in backpacking country.

Popular camps or camps near trail junctions may have established pit toilets with toilet seats, just like home. They will not have enclosures, so respect the privacy of the occupant. In one camping area an otherwise intelligent hiker pitched his tent about 10 feet from a public toilet. He sure took care of *his* problem, but precluded the use of the toilet by other hikers. Most public toilets of this type are located in dense stands of trees. You might look or inquire when arriving at a popular campsite.

Most mountain campsites are a wide spot in the trail that will accommodate one or two tiny tents, or more frequently they take the form of a semiflat spot near a tiny stream. Sites will *not* have established toilets.

In these locations it is worth the effort to try to locate a downed horizontal tree, not over one foot thick and about 1 to 1½ feet off the ground. If you locate this treasure, you have found your toilet seat. Break off the few branch stubs that might annoy you, leaving one vertical stub remaining, over which you may place your roll of toilet paper. Under the backside of your toilet seat dig a hole in the ground with a sharp rock or stick. Engineers and former bombardiers will do this with more precision than philosophers. Mount your edifice just like at home. When done, carefully cover your wastes and toilet paper with the soil dug out of the hole. One desert authority says to burn the used toilet paper. Perhaps in the arid desert paper doesn't decompose quickly, so this seems reasonable; however, in most areas it's superfluous since paper is essentially cellulose and will decompose quickly in damp earth, the same as the wood from which it came. I would not recommend lighting a match back in the woods during the dry season; you might ignite more than just your toilet paper.

If you plan to camp at the area for more than one night, or if you are with another couple, dig a deeper and longer hole and fill in a little at a time as needed.

My former scout troop of 25 to 30 boys carried a small one-pound shovel for the purpose of digging and filling in the latrine. When you finally break camp totally fill in the latrine and place a rock or branch over the spot to help hold the soil in place. I would suggest always bringing the toilet paper back with you and replacing it inside the plastic bag safely within your pack.

Many wilderness areas will be devoid of trees but may have a surplus of rocks. A very simple latrine in this situation can be created by selecting a lonesome area and overturning a basketball-size rock, then using the depression under the rock as your latrine. Dig out the depression a little deeper. When done, cover your wastes with earth you dug out, and carefully and gently replace the rock back into its depression.

If there are no trees and no basketball-size rocks, the basic latrine in this situation is known as a "cathole." Dig a hole in the soil with a sharp rock or your boot heel and when done cover with the soil dug out of the hole. Hopefully none of us will leave little papered piles out in the open along the trail or in potential campsites to plague fellow hikers.

Watering Trees

When urinating along the trail, find a bush or tree to your liking located well away from the trail. In the Tetons I once encountered a large party strung along the trail with guards posted up and down trail from where one of their anointed was urinating. Possibly the club treasurer or club sponsor had to go. Mighty impressive.

If your campsite is on or near a ledge or cliff, there is merit in rigging a taut safety line around your tent about stomach high and about body length away from the edge of the ledge. Thus, if you have to get up during the night to go the rope will remind you not to go all the way. Even on level ground it is good practice to decide where you are going to go during the night. One simple system is for one partner to go a few feet to the right of the tent and the other partner a few feet to the left of the tent. This simple exercise in communication will avoid muddy feet.

It's in the Bag

Another practical word. Always keep toilet paper inside a plastic bag. Absolutely nothing is as useless and frustrating as a rain-soaked roll of toilet paper. Still another thought: hang onto your toilet paper as cylindrical objects love to roll downhill out of your grasp at the exact moment when need is greatest.

Newcomers to backpacking sometimes try to conceal their toilet anxiety for several days. It's understandable. Novices can be easily recognized by their haggard expression, poor appetite, and glazed eyeballs. We all have to eliminate our wastes, and we all know it, so why be coy?

Equipment needed under this chapter consists of proper respect for *our* streams and lakes, a healthy attitude toward *our* clean campsites and trails, and a half roll of toilet paper for two people for one week, securely enshrined in a plastic bag.

Beginning
Backpack
Hikes

Learn to Live Out of Your Pack

By now you are probably looking ahead to your
first backpack and are wondering where to hike. A
few suggestions may be helpful.

On your first backpack you may wish to hike along
relatively horizontal roads or trails with very little, if
any, gain in altitude. The main idea is to learn to live
out of your pack and to learn to use your admittedly
meager equipment.

First Backpack from a Car Camp

One of my first backpacks was from a family car camp
in a state park to a low grassy hilltop less than one-
half mile away. Connie and I had noted the area on
previous walks from camp and had eaten a picnic
lunch in the exact spot we planned to camp. So you
might say we had done some *advance planning* and
were *generally familiar with the area*. I would not
begin to suggest you take off for some wild, remote
spot on your first backpack. You might not come
back.

Our base camp was a paid campsite in the state park.
We assembled our packs and food bags, which had
been prepacked at home in preparation for our adventure. Leaving after lunch, we hiked over to the
grassy campsite and pitched our tent, setting up house-
keeping for the night. A simple one-pot supper was

cooked, using the butane Gaz stove and dehydrated foods.

Dessert was instant pudding premixed at home with powdered milk. Actually, the whole meal was simply: add water, mix, stir frequently, and eat out of cups. Empty plastic one-gallon bleach bottles filled with drinking water had been lugged up earlier, as the campsite did not have a source of water.

As the evening turned to night, Connie and I put on our down jackets to ward off the chill and smiled at the hundreds of lanterns glaring from the crowded campsite below. Our hill was ours alone. Sleep was slightly slow in coming, as we were acutely aware of every sound and conscious that we were out and alone—a natural feeling that probably goes back to man's origin. Eventually we fell asleep.

Breakfast was cold cereal with powdered milk eaten in our tent. We didn't spill anything on our sleeping bags, as we had been alerted to be cautious.

The strangest experience was going to the bathroom out in the open. Rather tense. A hole was dug with a stick, carefully covered, and a rock rolled over the spot.

After a simple lunch we packed up all our gear and backpacked the one-half mile back to our base camp. Our initial backpack experience had come off without a hitch, and most importantly, Connie and I felt we had accomplished a rather meaningful step in our lives.

Hike Between Public and Private Camp

On another beginning backpack we located a private campground about three miles from a state park and paid for campsites at both locations. We drove to the state campground on a Friday night and in the manner of veterans pitched our mountain tent and went to sleep.

Saturday morning we cooked breakfast, washed dishes (two cups, two spoons, two pots) and packed up. Then we hiked over rolling roads to the private campground and set up camp on a ridge not acces-

sible by car. Lunch was simple. Supper was a dehydrated beef stew prepared in one pot. All we did
was add water, boil, stir, and eat. Pot was cleaned and
water heated for tea. Our shared tea bag yielded four
cups, not quite up to our record nine cups of fairly
recognizable tea from one tea bag at Roche-A-Cri, Wisconsin.

Saturday evening was pleasant on our ridge although
the ridiculously overcrowded private campground below doubled our determination to become proficient at
backpacking so that eventually we could confidently
handle more remote and less-crowded locations.

Sunday morning was disappointing, as it rained and
we had planned to cook our breakfast over a wood fire.
We improvised and cautiously arranged our gear so
that we could set up our butane Gaz stove inside our
tent in the front vestibule. It was the first time we
had cooked inside our tiny tent, an experience that
made us both rather apprehensive, but we rationalized
that if mountain climbers could cook in their tents we
could cook in ours. The basic problem is the potential
for spilling the pot of food and perhaps singeing hair
over the gas flame. Like many fears, neither material-
ized.

Since it was still raining after breakfast, we followed
an old Eskimo adage and "didn't fight nature," but
rather, went back to sleep. When we woke the rain
was over. This is a good point to remember. I have
noticed with interest that many pouring rains at 6 A.M.
have stopped by 7, 8, or 9 A.M. It's worthwhile to
be patient and delay your departure for a few hours
on the chance that the rain will stop. We delayed our
departure sufficiently to allow sun and wind to dry out
our tent so that the backpacking weight would be reduced. By shaking raindrops off the tent, the drying
out process was speeded up. The camp was packed
up and we hiked back to our base camp for a late
lunch.

Our backpack adventure had been successfully extended to two nights in a mountain tent and we had
survived a moderate rain.

Drinking Water for Waterless Sites

Waterless backpack campsites may be stocked with water carried in rinsed-out plastic one-gallon bleach bottles. Any residual bleach will not harm your drinking water since bleach is basically chlorine, which is the same chemical used to purify your city drinking water. Neighbors will save empty bleach bottles for you if they know you need them.

Cache (conceal and protect) your water supply a day in advance of your hike. Allow one gallon of water per person per day, plus water carried in water bottles. This will be sufficient for cooking and drinking, but will require sparse dishwashing. Dishes may be wiped out with bunches of grass and rinsed with a tiny bit of water. If on an overnight or weekend hike you must wash, rinse, do the laundry, take a Saturday night bath, etc., plan on two gallons of water per person per day. I've never operated under such a luxurious system. Being frugal with water is a challenge. Compared to supporting a dishwashing, clothes washing, toilet-flushing household, the water needs of one or two persons out camping are quite minimal. Most of your initial backpacks will be near roads so water supply is not too difficult to arrange in advance.

Home on the Range

On still another initial backpack one of our neighbors knew a dairy farmer five miles outside town who agreed to permit us to camp in one of his wooded fields. We stocked water in advance and determined which lanes were okay for hiking and which lanes belonged to his cows. Looking back on this adventure, the five miles seemed to go on forever. Also, not all the cows got the word we were to camp in *our* field and they were to camp in *their* field.

If you were to seek permission for camping on ranch or farmland, I would suggest you inform the farmer you will cook with your butane stove. This will put his mind at ease about potentially disastrous fires.

Farm people have a deep love for and pride in their land, so leave the campsite in such a way that no one would ever know you camped there. The ultimate compliment is to meet the farmer later and have him say, "When are you going camping? I thought you were coming in last weekend but when I drove over to the field no one had been there." Needless to say, we would have been most welcome again by the farmer; I never checked with the cows.

By *slowly* building up your mileage and expertise on initial backpacks you will avoid the classic mistake of discouragement caused by hiking too far too soon.

Selecting Backpacking Areas

When the rudiments of backpacking have been mastered to your satisfaction and you begin to feel at ease, you'll wish to extend your hikes to local county and state parks, or perhaps a state forest. If a national park or forest is near you, it will have many trails of varying degrees of difficulty.

Sunset Magazine has published travel books on specific Western states, and they may help you decide on certain areas within a state that seem more interesting than others to you. Once you have determined where you want to go, you could write for trail maps from regional or district forest-ranger offices in that area.

After a specific route has been selected from a trail map, you should purchase contour maps of the exact area you will be hiking. Contour (topographical) maps may be obtained from certain bookstores and most camping stores. For example, in the heart of downtown Chicago, Brentanno's bookstore sells contour maps of trails in the Teton Mountains. This fact has always struck me as being incongruous with the formal business community surrounding the bookstore.

In fact it is possible to obtain contour maps of just about any spot in the U.S.A., including the area where you live. For maps east of the Mississippi River, write:

U.S. Geological Survey, Washington, D.C. 20242. For maps west of the big river write: U.S. Geological Survey, Federal Center, Denver, Colorado 80225. A free index is available on request so you may select a specific contour map of an area within the state where you plan to hike. While you are at it, order the map covering your home town. We found our home street, school, church and park shown on the contour map that included Woodstock, Illinois.

The advantage of a contour map is that you may compare the trail map with the contour map and all the ups and downs of the trail will be shown in interesting detail, which may either sharpen your enthusiasm or stand your hair on end. At least you will know what to expect, or avoid, and may plan accordingly. Maps are fun to study in the winter, as you plan your next summer's mini backpacking "expedition."

There are many fine books describing interesting trails suitable for short or long backpacks. For example, an inexpensive hiking map of the Tetons, with the trail mileages given in tenths of a mile, may be obtained by writing to the Historical Society, Jackson, Wyoming. Some national forests and most national parks will have books, pamphlets, or maps describing trails within their boundaries. Some are free, some are not.

Backpack Hikes May Be Planned in Different Manners

Yo-Yo routes lead to camp and return along the same route. Many weekend hikes are of this nature. This type of backpack may be made more exciting by increasing the distance to camp to include two days going there plus a one-day-long hike back. Some hikes have a low trail mileage but are so vertical in nature that you'll have your work cut out for you. Other longer flatter routes are easy by comparison.

In search of a short two-day weekend hike, Connie and I ascended 3,000 feet of switchbacks on 2.7 trail miles in three hours; didn't like the rock-walled imprisoned lake and hiked back down the 2.7 steep miles. We drove to another trail and descended about 1,500 feet along two twisting miles of trail. Our "short" hike turned into 7.4 tough miles just getting there, but it was worth it. No other hiker was out in the light snow; we were alone, snug and safe within our tiny tent.

Our tent frosted that night and when we woke it was as if decorators had been working all night. Ice crystals sparkled from the inside walls of our tent and from the quiet snow outside. Silent flittering birds chased one another around the tiny steaming lake. By Sunday noon the snow and magic were gone and so were we.

Circular routes are a lot of fun and work well on a three- or four-day weekend. For variety try reversing your route to a favorite meadow, ridge, river or lake. Quite a few variations are possible. Circular routes enable you to become familiar with a geographic area larger than Yo-Yo routes. Within a circular route you will discover spots to which you may wish to return at a later date to spend several quiet days. Tom and I hiked a 33-mile circular route from Sunrise at Mt. Rainier, to Mystic Lake, to James Lake, and back to Sunrise. Each hike segment took one day, including a 2 ½-hour drive each way to the national park from our home in Issaquah, Washington.

Put-in and Pick-up routes are quite exciting. You are driven to, or "put-in" at the starting point and then backpack linearly across to a "pick-up" point on a certain date and time. This technique is well suited to the Cascade Mountains of Washington and other mountain areas. The technique is widely practiced in canoe camping. Both backpacker and pickup driver will usually spend the week worrying if they'll all meet at the pickup point at the correct time on the correct date.

This technique could be combined with one-half the family spending the week at a tent base camp, or in a cottage in the general pickup vicinity. In this manner both factions within a family get to do what they wish. On this type of trip you may wish to allow

WHERE TO GO BACKPACKING

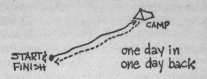

CAMP

START & FINISH

one day in
one day back

YO-YO TRIP

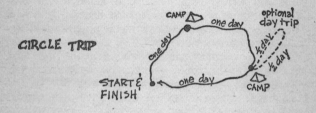

CAMP one day

optional
day trip

CIRCLE TRIP

one day

½ day

½ day

START & FINISH

one day

CAMP

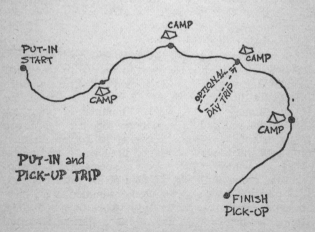

CAMP

PUT-IN
START

CAMP

CAMP

OPTIONAL
DAY TRIP

CAMP

PUT-IN and
PICK-UP TRIP

FINISH
PICK-UP

one additional day's time and food just in case bad weather is encountered. You'll be 100% on your own and fairly deep into wilderness on extended trips of this nature, so be sure you know which end is up before you start.

Dick and I hiked about 38 to 40 miles in four days on a trip of this nature. We had allowed five days, and rather than cool our heels at the trailend for one day, we hiked the planned two-day 16-mile final segment in one day and hitched a ride home with a family who finished their hike at the same time we finished ours.

I had rented boots, as my own boots had delaminated and were being repaired. A massive heel blister began about two miles out. First heel blister I ever had. We taped the hot spot, which prevented breakage, but the pain going uphill was so horrible that we considered turning back. About four miles out Dick had the brainstorm that we exchange left boots. Sure enough, his boot fit me and mine fit him. We finished the remaining 36 miles in little or no pain. The blister never did break, thanks to the tape. It was about 1 by 1½ inches across. Magnificent!

Spring and Fall Hikes

As you become familiar with an area and more certain of your growing ability, you may wish to extend your hiking season into spring and fall. These seasons are really the most beautiful. I enjoy late spring and early summer in the snowy mountains. Somehow mountains and snow seem to go together. Once you have extended your backpacking to cooler weather, you probably won't be satisfied until you have tried at least one winter camp. This is a specialized skill outside the scope of this book. One of my former scouts, Pat Cooney, now at West Point, summed it up nicely: after his first winter camp he woke on a sparkling, sunny five-degree day, sat up with a startled look and said, "My God, I'm alive."

Physical Conditioning and Mental Attitude

Conditioning is an attitudinal problem as much as a physical one. You get to the point of believing in your own abilities by successfully experiencing a series of increasingly difficult backpacks over a period of years. Good trip planning, knowing how to get the most out of your meager equipment, *the ability to improvise,* and skilled, pleasant companions all help make backpacking a pleasure. *When no one has to be told what to do, you have arrived.*

Once Tom and I were picking our way down a fairly steep, rocky section of trail, from Mystic Lake down along Carbon Glacier, in Mt. Rainier National Park, when we came upon a heavy-set young lady of about 20 years old, struggling very slowly upward. Her expression, boots, and gear suggested that she was new to backpacking. We had passed a hiking group or club about one-half hour earlier and concluded that the club had solved the new-hiker problem by abandoning the young lady in mid-trail.

That is no way to teach, learn, or, more importantly, to enjoy backpacking. Solo backpacking could deteriorate into a solo emergency situation rather quickly. Around Holland, Michigan, there is a saying, "Two heads are better than one, even if one is a cabbage head."

How Long Will It Take?

Warm Up First

To provide you with some yardstick to measure how far you can hike in one day, let's look at different terrain and conditions. In any hiking situation the tendency is to want to get there right away. If you can curb this normal eager attitude and *start out slowly,* you will avoid cramped shin and calf muscles that may ache for hours or days afterward. *Slow starts are the only way to begin any hike,* as they allow your muscles to warm up, permitting your body to become adjusted to the high energy being placed upon it. Slow starts are analogous to the athletes' "warm up" exercises prior to the main event.

During the first hour or so of your hike, both you and your pack feel strange. This is normal. During your first rest stop pull up your socks, readjust your boot laces, hitch up your shorts, add or remove clothing, smooth out a shirt lump, and adjust pack shoulder-strap length. Perhaps the bellyband is a bit loose or tight. Adjust it. Try to eliminate small annoyances which have a way of growing bigger. You'll feel very tired. This is normal. Initial intense fatigue passes within a few hours as your body adjusts to environment, load, climate and altitude. One authority states that this adjustment may take several days. Our family usually "gets with it" in a few hours.

Hiking on Level Ground

On level ground the Army figures 2½ trail miles per hour based on 50 minutes of hiking and 10 minutes of continuous rest. (The probable origin of the 10-minute break.) I do not recommend the concept of 10 minutes of continuous rest after 50 minutes of hiking, as heated muscles and tendons cool off and stiffness sets in. Thus each beginning-hike segment becomes difficult for the hiker who must "warm up" all over again, including the pain of restretching muscles and tendons. The moaning and groaning of Army units resuming a march was not all mythical. A far better procedure is to take brief rests of one or two minutes after some demanding point on a hike, or when a stream presents itself for a water break. Leave your pack on, unfasten your bellyband, get off your feet, and lean back into your pack to get the weight off your body. Swish a swallow of water around in your mouth, or in hot weather take a salt tablet about every hour or two with your swallow of water.

Don't bitch! It is totally demoralizing. Martyrs are unwelcome hike companions. Do factually mention "hot spots" on your heel or toe and apply adhesive tape directly over the potential blister before blisters develop and break. In short, on a brief break, catch your breath, enjoy the view, enjoy a swallow of water, tape a potential blister, and then move on.

I do agree with a rate of travel of 2½ trail miles per hour on fairly level ground. Thus a five-mile hike requires two hours, a 10-mile hike requires four hours, but curiously a 20-mile hike will take less than eight hours as a rhythm is built up on longer hikes, and few rests are needed or taken. Physiologically, I suppose the body is functioning at peak performance.

Hiking Uphill

On ascending grades, in foothills and mountain switchbacks, you can figure on one trail mile per hour. This is very practical for planning purposes; three trail miles uphill equals three hours. On gentle grades you will do better, but on continuous, hour-after-hour steep switchbacks you'll rarely exceed one trail mile per hour.

Connie and I exchange leads at each uphill switchback. The leader stops and waits for the follower to pass and take over the lead. The five- to ten-second standing rest for the leader is appreciated. The follower gets a psychological boost by becoming the leader and no longer has to inhale trail dust; also, the leader's view is better. Somewhere between switchbacks we usually take a standing break for a few seconds to look at the scenery, or to proudly look back upon the altitude gained. Sometimes we flop down along the trail for a few seconds after a demanding stretch, not necessarily on each switchback, but by mutual agreement. A tree shaded spot on the trail can be very persuasive. You'll know. Use the rest to enjoy the view. You will have earned it.

A slow, steady plodding pace going uphill is superior to "rush and collapse." Connie and I frequently pass and maintain our lead over much younger people who rush by one moment and then collapse along the trail a little later on. One young man literally vomited on the trail from self-induced exhaustion. In defense of our young man, his party carried all heavy canned goods, as that is all they could afford. One member of the four-man group wore tennis shoes although the trail was partially snow-covered. The following day when Connie and I were having fun glissading down snowy slopes on our boots, the sick young man dragged his body around camp. Plod, don't rush, and plod steadily.

Heel blisters occur going uphill if your heel moves up and down too much inside your boot. Avoid walking on the ball of your foot with heel off the ground; walk flat-footed and you'll have a better grip on the ground and may avoid heel blisters. You'll also induce less stress in muscles and tendons. Climbing books refer to this as "slab walking" technique. Try it!

A word on heart pounding. In order to sustain life your heart must beat. As physical demands increase your heartbeat will become more powerful; if it didn't, you couldn't meet the physical demands. This is not unusual, it is normal. A slow, plodding, steady uphill pace permits your heart to beat at a regular pace matching your energy output.

Adaptive Metabolism

Going uphill you'll huff and puff, naturally, as your body requires more oxygen. You'll probably breathe through your mouth, it's normal. Since your body processes more oxygen, it will give off more water vapor. Sweat will run into your eyes, that's why you'll tie a bandana around your forehead; your nose will drip (no you don't have a cold), and your arms will glisten. You're a beautiful creature, created in the image of God, and functioning in a perfectly normal manner. Over a period of time your whole metabolism will adapt to the load you are carrying and particularly to the outdoors. You'll feel, and be, vitally alive. Enjoy the feeling; you're becoming part of your wilderness environment. You're sharing and experiencing the aliveness of Man.

When returning home it will take several hours for your body to reduce its temperature setting. Your house will seem too hot and you'll feel a power that seems out of place indoors. This is the same phenomenon that propels people to dance after a full day of skiing. Collapse, yes; quit, never! Your metabolism will adjust in a few hours to your less physically demanding indoor environment; then you'll collapse.

Checkup or Autopsy?

With all the huffing and puffing we have described, it might be an excellent idea to find out what kind of physical shape you are in before beginning strenuous hikes. Only an autopsy will reveal your condition after a hike you couldn't complete. A physical checkup each year is comforting, to say the least. Adult leaders in scouting are required to have a physical examination before participating in strenuous physical activities or when attending long-term camps. Makes sense, doesn't it?

My doctor tells me I have the blood pressure and heartbeat of a 22-year-old, although he didn't say in what condition. How about you? Wouldn't you like to know where you stand before high energy demands are placed upon you?

It really isn't fair to expect your wife to carry you home; some wives might just leave you collapsed in the middle of the trail, cash in your life insurance and take up tango dancing with your business partner. I hope this thought will sustain you up the trail and down the trail and to your doctor's office.

Hiking Downhill

On descending grades you can figure about 2½ trail miles per hour, the same as for level hiking. Down-grades are deceiving since they are partially down and partially up. On the pure down segment you might make three trail miles per hour, but on the up segment you might drop back to one trail mile per hour.

The Lesser Evil: Uphill or Downhill

A favorite item of conversation among hikers is which is more demanding: uphill or downhill hiking? Uphill obviously requires more energy output, but downhill requires constant slowing, or checking, that is painfully felt just above the knees. The worst downhill I can recall was in the Tetons, from Alaska Basin down to Phelps Lake, about a 4,200-foot descent, that came on the end of a 12- to 14-mile day of up and down hiking. That particular downhill reduced me to rubble. Finally, after descending, we encountered a trail sign that read, "1 mile to Phelps Lake." That was one Texas-size mile.

Going uphill your lungs burn and you want to collapse as you can't lift your leg another step; going downhill your legs tremble and turn to rubber and actually get out of control. You'll rarely stumble going uphill, but you'll rarely not stumble going downhill. Beware of a twisted ankle on the downhill we're-going-home segment of the hike. This is not the time to abandon caution, although you probably will; most people do, and downhill is where most accidents occur. Downhill seems easy, but actually it is quite demanding.

Loose gravel, pine needles, leaves and grass are especially unstable on a descent. Sightseeing going downhill seems to end up with toes bumping into uphill trail banks or boots slipping over the edge on the downhill side. Enjoy the view, but watch where you are walking.

Conditioning Hikes

For initial conditioning hikes five level miles without pack would take about two hours and might be something you would want to do for a few weekends in a row, working the mileage up to say ten miles in four hours by the end of the month. After that, your first backpack might be as little as three miles to as much as five miles. I would not suggest going any farther.

Many hikers plan hike segments between five to eight miles per day. It depends on altitude gain and how far apart campsites are located. Most established trail camps are six to ten miles apart. In the mountains our family has hiked from six to thirteen miles per day, which might average about eight to ten miles per day. Hold down the initial mileage so that your overall experience is a good feeling. No need to discourage yourself.

Fun Hikes

Some rather exotic hiking times may be of interest to you.

In Illinois, one fast 20-mile hike on a fairly level trail, without pack, required six hours, including time to eat lunch. In the Tetons, one 20-mile hike, consisting of five steep miles of 4,000-foot ascent without pack, and 15 fast miles of 4,300-foot descent with pack, took 10 hours. In Stehekin, Washington, one very steep 18-mile hike with five slow miles of 3,000-foot ascent and 13 fast miles of 6,000-foot descent, with pack, took nine hours. In the Glacier Peak area, Washington, one 16-mile, 4,500-foot descending hike, with pack, required six hours.

All these hikes were taken on the last day of camping, homeward bound, admittedly way too fast, with the 16- and 18-mile hikes resulting in toe blisters, above and beyond the heel blister previously described.

Sometimes it's fun to probe your own limits just to see what you can do. Blisters heal; memories are forever.

Clothing and Equipment List for a Two-Person Team

Checklist for Two Backpackers

A comprehensive list of all clothing and equipment suggested in this book is included as a guide and checklist for two people for backpacks of two days to two weeks. Price and weight of gear is given for 1974.

The following specific example is for a hike of seven days; for shorter or longer trips, or additional people, merely modify the total amount of food, toilet paper, and spare fuel cartridges as described later.

Clothing and Equipment for Two People for Seven Days

Each backpacker is wearing: $35 hiking boots, socks, undershorts, trousers, optional T-shirt, short or long-sleeved shirt, sun glasses, bandana, $3.50 scout pocket knife, 67¢ scout screw-top match-safe filled with large paraffin-coated self-striking wooden matches, $3 compass, contour map of area, $1 Sierra cup on your belt, today's trail food in your pocket, driver's license, gas credit card, car key, house key, and cash-coin-check.

Each backpacker is carrying: $10 to $36 pack and frame (about 3¼ pounds total), $25 Dacron mummy bag (4¼ pounds), stuff sack or plastic sack of spare clothing [socks, underwear, optional T-shirt, $3 long-sleeved Orlon (6-ounces) sweater, $25 down jacket (16 ounces), $12 nylon rain jacket with hood (10 ounces)], stainless steel spoon, filled 2½-cup plastic water bottle (22 ounces), $4 foam pad 1½ inches thick, full length

173

(1¾ pounds), 15-foot coil of one-eighth-inch nylon line to compress and tie foam pad (1½ ounces).

Both backpackers share in carrying: $30 to $140 two-person mountain tent (4½ pounds), tent poles and bag (1 pound), tent pins and bag (7 ounces), 50-foot coil of one-eighth inch nylon line (4½ ounces), nesting 1½-quart and 1-quart cooking pots each with bail handle (9 ounces), nylon pot scrubber, $9 butane stove including filled fuel cartridge (1½ pounds), spare fuel cartridge (10 ounces), 1-gallon collapsible plastic water jug with screw top (2 ounces), 1 nylon net bag (½ ounce), ½ roll toilet paper in plastic bag, first-aid supplies and first-aid manual in plastic bag (8 ounces), one-inch candle stub (½ ounce), 1 tiny flashlight with fresh bulb and alkaline battery (1½ ounces), 8 breakfasts in plastic bag, 8 lunches in plastic bag, 8 suppers in two plastic bags, one plastic staple bag of individually bagged sugar, powdered cream, instant tea, and freeze-dried coffee.

Personal items carried by individual backpackers: Prescription medication, paperback book, sanitary napkins or preferably tampons, camera, spare film, tripod, sliver of soap, hiking shorts, fishing rod, swim suit, etc. I remember hand carrying a movie camera on a Rocky Mountain backpack in 1969 and I wouldn't do that again.

Shorter Hikes and Longer Hikes

Shorter hikes of two or three days would not require the spare fuel cartridge. Be sure fresh fuel cartridge is in stove when starting all hikes. I would suggest omitting spare undershorts and T-shirt. Food would decrease to two or three days' supply, plus one additional day of food. Hold all other items constant.

Longer hikes of up to two weeks would increase the amount of food based on the specific number of days, plus one additional day of food. On the basis of two fuel cartridges per two people per week, bring three spare fuel cartridges plus fresh cartridges in stove. On the basis of a half roll of toilet paper per two people per week, bring either one full roll or two half rolls, whichever packs easier for you. I would suggest carrying one spare flashlight battery and bulb. Always start a hike with fresh battery and bulb in your flashlight.

Pack Volume Critical

Longer hikes require more pack volume to hold the additional bags of food. Depending on the size of your pack this may mean you will have to omit a few items from equipment normally carried on shorter trips. Some candidates for omission are: camera, spare film cartridges, tripod, collapsible water jug, sugar, powdered cream, plastic mixing bottle for salad dressing, paperback book, hiking shorts, swim suit, and fishing rod. You *could* lash your fishing rod securely to the outside of your pack with nonslipping leather boot laces to provide more room inside your pack. You really don't need a swim suit. Instead of spare film consider one roll of 36 exposures in the camera and one spare 36-exposure roll, then question the need for the spare roll.

You may also wish to consider omitting tent poles, but be a realist and have something specific in mind to hold up your tent that will be practical and not theoretical. A compromise is to take front poles, but omit rear poles, which being shorter are easier to improvise from downed branches, ice axe, or pack frame.

You also have one other effective volume-saving device available: consider each food item on a volume basis (e.g., dessert could be one small chocolate bar per person in lieu of bulky instant pudding or cooked fruit, etc.). Good luck.

Lighter-Weight Hikes

Lighter-weight hikes are certainly possible and the following items are candidates for substitution or omission with corresponding weight reduction based on a *two-person team:*

	Maximum	Minimum
Omit front & rear tent poles	16 oz.	
Omit rear tent poles only		4 oz.
Use short 1½ inch-thick foam pads		18 oz.
Use short ¼ inch-thick foam pads	38 oz.	
Use 3 lb. 10 oz. down bag		20 oz.
Use 3 lb. 4 oz. down bag	32 oz.	
Omit 1 qt. pot	3 oz.	3 oz.
Substitute 2 cans instant freeze-dried ham for tuna	4 oz.	4 oz.
Substitute 2 chocolate bars for instant pudding	1 oz.	1 oz.
Omit sugar & Pream	6 oz.	6 oz.
Weight reduction, 2 people	100 oz.	56 oz.

Thus an average weight reduction of 6 pound 4 ounces to 3 pounds 8 ounces *per two persons* is possible; however, omitting tent poles can be problematic and shorter or thinner foam pads are not comfortable to either me or Connie, although they may suit your needs. (¼-inch pads insulate against ground cold, they do not provide comfort.)

I'd like a lesser weight mummy bag as this is one of the two largest possible weight reductions, but most down bags are designed for well-to-do thin people. I'm 5 feet 10 inches, weigh 195 pounds and wear jacket size 44. Good down bags that would fit me are either heavier than my dacron four-pound four-ounce total weight bag or are too hot for me. If I were thinner, I'd choose Sierra Designs "Superlight" at three pounds four ounces total weight with 27 ounces of down. Hopefully, you will fit a three-pound four-ounce total weight down bag. I wish I did.

Other items are not critical and can be altered, although one-pot meals become boring and omitting staples takes some of the joy out of eating. Chocolate bars are great, but with pudding I can make "almost" milk shakes. I agree with ham salad, but I enjoy tuna salad and shrimp salad.

As you see, further weight reduction gets into personal preference. Now that we have explored some of the pros and cons, you are free to make up your own list, weigh items, and choose the best overall weight-comfort-money relationship.

Larger Groups

Larger backpacking parties, up to eight people, will each wear or carry the same items as a two-person team. Equipment is the same on a per-person basis, except for the following five items:

1. Cooking pot sizes increase to one 4-quart and one 2-quart for the entire eight-person party.
2. First-aid supplies increase slightly.
3. Only one butane stove is required for the entire party.
4. Add a lightweight strong tarp to cover cooking-eating area. Suggest cotton 10-foot by 10-foot (2½ pounds) with tie tapes. Include 100 feet of ⅛-inch nylon line to rig the tarp.
5. Add latrine shovel (½ to 1 pound).

It can be seen that larger parties, up to eight people, are merely extensions of the basic two-person tent team with weight per person almost constant for all practical purposes. Odd-numbered parties are possible if one person owns a three-person tent; thus three, five, and seven-person parties will also fit the backpacking system described in this book.

Major Changes in Larger Groups

What then are the changes when hiking with a larger party? Major changes are: (1) cooking procedure where greater quantity of food is being prepared and greater probability of spilling exists, (2) distribution of equipment within packs (e.g., one person carries half of all breakfasts, another person carries half of all lunches, etc.), (3) concern for safety must increase, and (4) there are more people to assist in common tasks (e.g., one person rigs the cooking tarp, another feeds the fire, another prepares soup, etc.). This suggests that hikers with dissimilar skills would be most welcome.

To keep all this talent pointed in the same direction, an agreed-upon skilled leader is required for a smoothly functioning party. One of the major functions of a leader is to arrange for the buying and packaging of food. Merely packing up all gear in eight packs is fairly traumatic. Knowing who has what equipment requires ESP unless Jim takes care of the latrine, Betty is in charge of first aid, Bob rigs tarps, etc. In other words, assign hikers specific equipment responsibilities. If your group hikes regularly try rotating duties so that all members advance in skills.

Following a suggestion in *Going Light With Backpack or Burro* I bought a 25-pound-capacity fish scale with a hook to weigh disputed items in our net bag each morning when my sons and I hiked in the Tetons. Pack weight is a common source of disagreement, but when each person realizes that he is carrying essentially the same load as the other person, or an equitable load, tempers relax on a difficult ascent.

Greater Joy and Freedom Is With a Two-Person Team

I've backpacked with two, four, five, six, seven, and eight total people as a small group and up to 25 to 30 people as a large group. Generally, smaller groups are more fun for me than larger groups, and the smallest group is a two-person team.

As a two-person team you'll see more, do more, do it more leisurely, and far more joyfully, and that's what this book has been all about.

REFERENCE BOOKS, RELATED BOOKS & SUPPLY SOURCES

Suggested Reference Books for Backpackers

Boy Scout Handbook
Boy Scouts of America
(most department stores)

See: 2nd Class First Aid, Sanitation, Fire Making, Cooking Fires (especially small one). Good illustrations.

Mountaineering, the Freedom of the Hills
Harvey Manning,
The Mountaineers
Seattle, Washington
2nd Edition, 1967

See: Snow, Ice, First Aid, and read and understand "Balance" on a slope.

Going Light with Backpack or Burro
Sierra Club, 1962

See: Wilderness Traveling, Food and Cooking, Women, Mountain Medicine (magnificent book for overall feeling of backpacking).

Ropes, Knots and Slings for Climbers
Walt Wheelock
La Siesta Press, 1967

See: Knots and Relative Strength of Knots (as a percent of rope strength).

Backpacking, One Step at a Time
Harvey Manning
REI Press, Seattle, 1972

See: Danger, When the Way Grows Rough, The New Ethic, (review of available camp equipment and clothing).

The Complete Walker
Colin Fletcher
Alfred A. Knopf
New York, 1971

See: A Sample Day in the Kitchen, The Kitchen in Action Under Special Conditions (in a tent)—(a most excellent book, especially "Pink Toe" tenting).

First Aid Merit Badge Book
Boy Scouts of America
(most department stores)

See: Bleeding, Mouth to Mouth Resuscitation, Shock, Heat Exhaustion, Bandages, Slings, Choking, Transport.

*Surviving the Unexpected
Wilderness Emergency*
Gene Fear
Survival Education Association
Tacoma, Washington 98445

An excellent book that should be read by all who enter wilderness areas and also plan to exit.

Mountaineering Medicine
Fred T. Darvill, Jr., M.D.
Skagit Mountain Rescue
Unit, Inc., P.O. Box 2,
Mt. Vernon, Washington
98273

Take this one-ounce booklet with you in your first-aid bag. Book costs $1 and proceeds go to rescue unit serving one of the areas in which I hike.

Related Books on Wilderness

Listening Point
Sigrud F. Olson
Alfred A. Knopf
New York, 1960

Poetic awareness of wilderness ecology, simplicity, excellent line drawings.

In Wildness is the Preservation of the World
Eliot Porter
Sierra Club-Ballantine
1967

Thoreau's prose and Porter's exquisite color photographs help us become aware of nature's subtle beauty.

Shining Trail
Iola Fuller
Popular Library
Eagle Books
New York

The Saulk-Fox Indian way of life (now known as "wilderness").

Sunset Books

Travel guides to: Pacific Northwest, Washington State, and other Western states. Will help you decide in which state to hike.

Exploring Mt. Rainier
Ruth Kirk
University of Washington
Press
Seattle, Washington, 1969

Details of backpacking routes and trail miles in an area of national interest.

Identification Books

Flowers, Trees, Rocks, Birds, Animals, etc.

*Supply Sources (items mentioned in book italicized)

Eddie Bauer
P.O. Box 3700
Seattle, Washington 98124

Manufacturer of excellent *down clothing* and down mummy bags *Boots*, packs, nylon two-person tents, cooking pots, butane stoves.

Recreational Equipment, Inc.
1525—11th Ave.
Seattle, Washington 98122

Manufacturer of REI down clothing and down mummy bags, *Dacron mummy bag, packs, boots, nylon two-person tents, nylon line, rain jacket, Sierra cup, one-quart cook pot, pint plastic water bottle, collapsible one-gallon jug, backpacking foods, butane stove.*

Sierra Designs
4th and Addison
Berkeley, California 94710

Manufacturers of excellent *down mummy bags, nylon two-person tents.* Down clothing.

Gerry Outdoor Equipment
Colorado Outdoor Sports
Corporation
P.O. Box 5544
Denver, Colorado 80217

Manufacturers of excellent down mummy bags, down clothing, *packs, nylon two- and three-person tents,* cloth materials, boots, cooking gear, butane stoves.

Holubar
Box 7
Boulder, Colorado 80302

Manufacturer of *excellent two-person nylon tents,* down clothing, down mummy bags, packs, boots, cook pots, butane stoves, packs.

Thomas Black & Sons
930 Ford Street
Ogdenburg, New York
13669

Cotton tarp, down clothing, down mummy bags, cook pots, packs.

Camp Trails
3920 W. Clarendon Avenue
Phoenix, Arizona 85019

Manufacturers of excellent packs, pack frames and *padded belly bands.*

Himalayan Industries
807 Cannery Row
P.O. Box 950
Monterey, California 93940

Manufacturer of excellent *pack-frames and packs.*

L. L. Bean, Inc.
Freeport, Maine

Cotton two-three-four-person tents, down bags, down clothing, packs, boots, cook pots, butane stoves, Sierra cup.

*These suppliers are known to me; there are undoubtedly many other fine suppliers not known to me.

Morsan
810 Route 17
Paramus, New Jersey 07652
(8 stores serving East, no mail order anymore)

Cotton two-three-four-person tents, Dacron mummy bags, hard aluminum wire tent pins, mosquito netting.

Boy Scout Distributors
(most department stores)

Replacement patrol cooking-kit pots, e.g., *four-quart pot, two-quart pot, scout knife, matchsafe, compass, books.*

Sears

Full-cut jeans, Pima cloth workshirts.

Wilson Foods

Canned freeze-dried meat, bacon bar, meat bar.

Pro-Vita Food
201 Myer Street
Chico, California 95926

Franola with mixed fruit and nuts.

ABOUT THE AUTHOR

CHARLES JANSEN lives in Issaquah, Washington, and is on the faculty of the University of Washington.

ABOUT THE ILLUSTRATOR

LINDA BENNETT lives in Berkeley, California. Her last work appeared in *The Well Body Book*.

BANTAM HAS BRUCE TEGNER BOOKS ! ! !

Bantam publishes Bruce Tegner books on self-defense and sport aspects of weaponless fighting skills. Buy them at your local bookstore or use the handy coupon below for ordering.

☐ KUNG FU AND TAI CHI   7819 $1.25

☐ COMPLETE BOOK OF JUKADO   8015 $1.25

☐ COMPLETE BOOK OF JUDO   8019 $1.25

☐ COMPLETE BOOK OF AIKIDO & HOLDS
   & LOCKS   8417 $1.25

☐ COMPLETE BOOK OF KARATE   8752 $1.25

How's Your Health?

Bantam publishes a line of informative books, written by top experts to help you toward a healthier and happier life.

Bantam Book Catalog

It lists over a thousand money-saving best-sellers originally priced from $3.75 to $15.00 —bestsellers that are yours now for as little as 50¢ to $2.95!

The catalog gives you a great opportunity to build your own private library at huge savings!

So don't delay any longer—send us your name and address and 10¢ (to help defray postage and handling costs).